Dogs' London

the city's best walks for dogs & their owners

Mary Scott

Published by Sigma Leisure – an imprint of
Sigma Press, 1 South Oak Lane, Wilmslow, Cheshire SK9 6AR, England.

British Library Cataloguing in Publication Data
A CIP record for this book is available from the British Library.

ISBN: 1-85058-558-X

Typesetting and Design by: Sigma Press, Wilmslow, Cheshire.

Cover photograph: Fred with ball, by David Berman.

Maps: Morag Perrott

Cartoons: Rebecca Harvey

Printed by: MFP Design and Print

Disclaimer: the information in this book is given in good faith and is believed to be correct at the time of publication. No responsibility is accepted by either the author or publisher for errors or omissions, or for any loss or injury howsoever caused. Only you can judge your own fitness, competence and experience.

Foreword

There is a rich tapestry of green space weaving its way throughout London. With Dogs' London in one hand and a lead in the other you will have two ideal companions to explore some of our Capital's best-kept secrets.

This thoroughly researched and humorous guide introduces twenty leafy walks away from the hustle and bustle of urban life. Some fascinating historical commentary is supplemented with easy-to-follow route descriptions, maps and details of all the facilities and amenities which you will find on your way. All the walks have been carefully planned to start and finish at a rail or tube station so you will be able to enjoy a congestion-free journey.

From tranquil river and canal corridors to regal Victorian parks, from enchanting ancient woodland to disused railways rich in wildlife, it is perhaps the sheer diversity and quality of green spaces on your doorstep which will amaze you. Your walks will string these spaces together like emeralds on a necklace, giving you the impression of a walk in the countryside whilst you are in the City.

But don't forget, this valuable resource is for everyone's enjoyment so please take along your poop scoop!

Simon Kemp
London Walking Forum

To my uncle Bob who loved green places and whose gift after his death paid for Fred, my maps, rucksack, walking boots, thermos and cagoul.

Preface

When I first bought Fred I took him morning and evening to the local park. These outings were the high spots of his day. I can't say they were mine. A couple of weeks throwing a ball across the same patch of fouled, scuffed grass in a smelly Upper Holloway dog enclosure and the novelty soon wore off. So I stuffed a large scale A to Z, plastic bags and a tennis ball into a knapsack and we set off to explore.

On each walk further and further from home I was amazed at how green London is. And how varied. You'd be hard put to find such a range of terrain in any one area of the countryside proper. It was a revelation to discover that we didn't need to quit the capital to discover walks which suited us both: we could reach them by Tube, for goodness sake!

What makes a good walk for a dog? Fred wants to run, sniff interesting smells, make new friends, roll in long grass, plop into muddy puddles, chase sticks or a ball and, in hot weather, have a dip in some water. The walks in this book all offer such delights.

But most people – me included – want a bit more. Scenery, for instance. London has acres and acres of heath and woodland and meadow and marsh and rivers and ponds; it has stunning views from the summits of hills and secluded spots in which you can forget the city around you exists. The last are my favourites. I like to hear birdsong, watch foxes and rabbits at play, see butterflies dipping through daisies and poppies in unmown hayfields and stroll beneath the green canopy of ancient trees in Fred's undemanding company.

I like too to know something of the background of the places I visit. So I have included snippets of history – both natural and man-made – of the terrain we crossed.

I also need to be sure Fred won't come to grief around the next corner; that we won't emerge from a wood onto a dual carriageway or into a playground full of kids screaming fit to tempt the most sober dog into a boisterous (and easily misconstrued) attempt to join the fun. I warn you of these and of other hazards. I mention pubs and open air cafes where you can eat and drink with your dog beside you. And I include poop scoop regulations wherever they apply – though really it's as well to pick up after your dog in every London open space. So many parks have closed their gates to dogs because of fouling; it would be a sad shame if any of us were instrumental in diminishing even further our right to enjoy the city's green oases. You don't need to buy a device to pick up your dog's dirt – all you need is the plastic bags with which most of us get landed anyway by the local supermarket. It's as easy to stuff a couple of them into your pocket as it is to snap on your dog's lead. Local authorities all over the capital are having serious headaches about dog fouling, yet you can cure them with a couple of plastic bags.

And I hope the authorities will look at the other side of the coin. Too many of them see dogs solely as a nuisance. But without Fred I wouldn't, as a single woman, feel comfortable in many of the places I've walked. He's not an aggressive dog, but I know he'd do his best to protect me if I were in trouble. And with Fred along I share common ground with the people I meet. In inner city open spaces, people with mutts on strings chat to me about their pets. In upmarket parkland, green-wellied gents greet me with, 'Good morning'. Dog owners help to make London's open spaces safe. Go to almost any park between 10 and 12 of a morning and you are not alone. There is another dog walker on the horizon.

Of course there are irresponsible dog owners – I heard about them from almost every organisation I contacted. What do we do about them? The one thing we don't do – in my view – is to ban dogs or insist they are on leads. Dogs which are used to running free and have plenty of exercise are not, barring a tiny number of deranged canines, dangerous dogs. Nor is their mess a health hazard if they are regularly wormed.

But it *is* unpleasant and unnecessary. And some people simply won't clean up. My preference would be to reintroduce dog licences. Over the last years Fred has given me far more pleasure than my television ever has. Why not charge people the price of a TV licence each year for owning a dog (with exemptions for pensioners and people on low incomes)? Why not use the revenue thus generated to employ dog wardens to patrol the streets to make sure everyone picks up after their dog?

And why doesn't every London borough introduce a blanket poop scoop requirement in all its parks? Forget the special dog areas, allow dogs to mix with people – and get seriously heavy with the owners who don't pick up after their pets.

Finally (particularly if you're planning to buy a dog, but haven't yet taken the plunge) a word about Fred's background. The Dogs' Home Battersea picked him up in the street when he was around two years old. When I bought him he had a vague notion of what 'Sit' meant, but that was it. He wasn't even house-trained.

Within a week he was clean indoors. Within two he came to a whistle. Within three we were on our travels. Apart from a tendency to bark his head off at loud-voiced men, people lurking behind bushes and feet (he'd probably been kicked) he hasn't put a paw wrong since. So if you are contemplating buying a dog, do think of a rescue one.

But whatever your brand of dog, I hope this book will inspire you to get out and about with him and sample the remarkable variety of 'countryside' we Londoners are lucky to have on our doorsteps. Oh – and if we run across each other on a green hillside or a heath or in a wood, do stop and say hello. Fred'll be the one with a tennis ball in his mouth.

Mary Scott

& Fred . . .

Contents

↑
to   Totteridge
Barnet

Finchley   Muswell
Hill   (14)

kingsbury   Golders   (7)
Green
Harrow   Hampstead
on the   (4)   Neasden   Heath
Hill
(5)   Hampstead   (1)
Wembley   (17)   Willesden   (6)

Greenford

(18)   Paddington   (2)

Acton   Kensington   (8)
Westminster
Chiswick
(13)   (15)
(9)   Barnes
Richmond   Putney

Richmond
Park   Wimbledon
Common
Streatham
Wimbledon

Mitcham

(12)   Morden

Croydon

Tottenham

 ③ Walthamstow

Wanstead

Finsbury
Park

Stratford ⑩   Manor
Park   ⑯

Hackney

Dagenham

Mile End

Stepney ⑲

R. Thames

Woolwich

Camberwell ⑳ Plumstead

Peckham

Brockley

Eltham

Dulwich

Crystal
Palace   Sydenham

South
Norwood

5 mls

Purley

Coulsdon
⑪

How To Use This Book

Dogs' London doesn't pretend to be comprehensive, there are far too many rewarding walks in the capital for that. What I have tried to do instead is to introduce you to some of our favourite excursions. And – to save you travelling miles and miles – I have included walks in most areas of the city.

My walks aren't designed to be followed slavishly from end to end. They are intended to give you a flavour of the terrain you might cover and to inspire you to select the kind of outing you like and which you know your dog will enjoy. Many of the walks are far longer than the average dog needs; you can pick and mix routes which suit your energy levels. All the walks begin and end at tube or BR stations. You can look these up in the index to work out a route near you: or look up your nearest park and take it from there. I've also indicated where you can go further afield than I have – mostly on waymarked trails.

With a few exceptions most of *my* walks are unwaymarked; because for me half the fun of walking is exploring. The most exciting discovery I've made is of London's rivers. If you'd asked me, before I started this book, to name the tributaries of the Thames, I could at a pinch have come up with the river Lee and the subterranean Fleet. Now I know of the Beam, the Brent, the Crane, the Duke of Northumberland's, the Hogsmill, the Longford, the Peck, the Pool, the Ravensbourne, the Roding, the Wandle; Beverley Brook, Bollo Brook, Dollis Brook, Folly Brook, Mayes Brook, Mutton Brook, Norbury Brook, Pymmes Brook, Yeading Brook; the Silk Stream; and Barking Creek. I've walked beside some of them but by no means all. You could, though.

Walk 1: Manor House to Alexandra Park

A charming walk for both dogs and owners, with very little road walking. Includes formal parks as well as remnants of the ancient 'wildwood' which once covered all of London. It follows Parkland Walk – a green corridor along an old railway line. Connects with Walks 3, 6, 7 and 14.

Route: Manor House to Finsbury Park, Highgate and East Finchley. Diversions to Arsenal, Drayton Park BR and Highbury Islington, Archway and Alexandra Park BR. Extension Walks to Bowes Park BR, Bounds Green and Wood Green. Also, a circular walk from Highgate.

Distance: 4½ miles. Extension to Wood Green, 2½ miles. Highgate Circular walk, 4 miles.

Facilities: Loos in Finsbury Park, Holloway Road, Highgate Wood, The Grove. Highbury Fields and Cherry Tree Wood. Seasonal cafes in Finsbury Park, Highgate Wood, The Grove, Highbury Fields and Cherry Tree Wood. Pubs with gardens along the route.

From Manor House cross Seven Sisters Road and enter Finsbury Park. Cross the broad carriageway ahead and release your dog. There are no restrictions on dogs in the park, although there are some (clearly marked) areas from which they are excluded. Turn left on a path between herbaceous borders, strike left at a gap in the border, turn right at a Peace Mile marker and walk the length of a rugby pitch. Follow a tarmac path to the left, then head across grass to a shelter.

The park is formally laid out in the Victorian manner. But:

> *Where lovingly both man and wife*
> *May take the evening air*
> *And London dames to dry their cloathes*
> *May hither still repair.*

That was Finsbury Park in an old ballad. In those days it was part of the forest of Middlesex. It was the playground of north London where City bands drilled and people practised archery. On it was built London's first theatre which was later removed and reconstructed on Bankside. The park still carries on the tradition of entertainment: it's a venue for rock concerts.

In those days it was part of the forest of Middlesex. The woods were felled with the best of intentions – to improve the health of the working classes. But at least one contemporary commentator had a few regrets. 'The wild wood of Hornsey,' he wrote, 'will be transformed into the pretty park of Finsbury, but those who can remember this last vestige of the forest land will sometimes sigh for the lost rusticity of the wood.'

At the shelter continue straight across the grass, with Seven Sisters Road to your left. In case you wonder who the seven sisters were: when the street was constructed in 1832 it led to seven trees on common land at Page Green. Legend grew, as legends do, that they were memorials to seven women. The opposite side of the busy road is lined with hotels. Who on earth, with all of London to choose from, would opt to stay in this grimy, northern corner of the capital? But perhaps, these days, the hotels provide B&B for the city's homeless people.

Turn right along the next tarmac path. Pass a cafe to your right and cross the western stretch of the carriageway. If you fancy a diversion, turn right along the carriageway (with your dog on the lead, there is traffic on the road and waterfowl on the lake) to inspect a sad section of the New River imprisoned behind iron railings at the north of the park. The New River isn't a real river. It was dug in the seventeenth century to supply fresh water to London. For most of its course it is now covered, but it surfaces again at Clissold Park (see Walk 3) and again in south Islington at New River Walk in Canonbury where dogs are not welcome. If you don't inspect the New River, take the path ahead which leads to a high, chain fence and an information board about Parkland Walk.

To reach Finsbury Park, Drayton Park BR, Arsenal and Highbury Islington

Turn left after the information board along the path beside the railway. There are wild lupins here and further on, in spring, snowdrops and crocuses. In summer, street people inhabit the benches and the barer patches of ground, stripped to the waist to

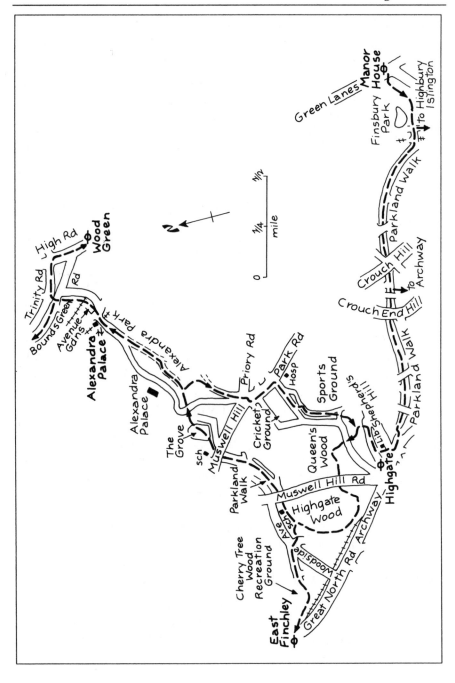

enjoy the sun; snakes of ash dripping from their cigarettes, cans of Special Brew in their hands. I expect they'll stop you and ask you for a cigarette.

When you hear traffic, put your dog on the lead and leave the Walk on Stroud Green Road. Turn left, cross the road to the right at the first lights, go left again across Station Place past Finsbury Park station (which has a subway and stairs) and right to reach Seven Sisters Road. Cross it, to go along St. Thomas's Road. In the near future you will be able to walk to Arsenal along a southern extension of Parkland Walk, the entrance to which will be at the top of St. Thomas's Road. For now continue along the road to find, to the right through an arched gate, the charming meadow of Gillespie Park. You can release your dog in here, but must clean up after him. And do remember that this delightful place is managed for wildlife – and is designated a site of metropolitan importance by the London Ecology Unit. Some parts are fenced to prevent dogs entering them, but the remainder is a refreshing slice of countryside with twisty paths leading between woodland and nettles from the open, un-mown grassland at the north. But perhaps the most remarkable fact about the park is that it was only created in 1981. Nature has worked hard since then to make a beautiful oasis in an area of Islington where peaceful green places are few and far between – so don't let your dog rush around too much and destroy the idyll (and upset the wildlife.) The twisty path takes you to Gillespie Road.

To reach Arsenal

Turn right and the station is a few metres further.

To reach Drayton Park BR

After Arsenal, pass the Islington Ecology Centre on the right (when the extension of Parkland Walk is complete, the lane beside the Centre will be its southern exit) and follow Drayton Park to the station.

To reach Highbury Islington

At Arsenal station cross to Highbury Hill and follow the quiet road to the Victorian clock at the top of Highbury Fields. Turn right down Church Path and release your dog. Put him on the lead to cross

Baalbec Road. Highbury Fields, on which you are now walking, is the largest open space in Islington: a flat, mown field with no restrictions on dogs. Cross its length staying far enough from Highbury Place for your dog to be safe from traffic. At the swimming pool put him on the lead and cross Holloway Road to Highbury Islington station. It has stairs to the BR line and escalators to the tube.

In the future you may be able to walk from the Ecology Centre to Highbury Islington on yet another extension of Parkland Walk. Local people are campaigning to open up a corridor of railway land which will fetch up in Robin Yard, to the west of Highbury Swimming Pool. I hope they succeed.

To continue on the main route

From Finsbury Park cross the blue and red bridge ahead over the railway and turn right onto Parkland Walk. There are no restrictions on dogs and the route is fenced apart from where paths lead into it from nearby streets. There is no requirement to pick up after your dog either and no dog mess bins, which I consider a pity – there is a great deal too much mess on either side of the path. If your dog tends towards aggression to other dogs in narrow places, or chases cyclists or joggers, then be warned that in some of the Walk's north western stretch it is a single file affair. But here it is a wide, airy track. It follows the course of the railway which, until 1970, connected Finsbury Park to Alexandra Palace and, unlike Finsbury Park itself, has no formality at all. Wild plants and trees flourish. Foxes live here, as do bats. In 1985 even a muntjac was spotted. The muntjac is a miniature deer, introduced from China earlier this century. It makes a barking noise – yes, honest! – and I've only ever seen one in Hertfordshire woodland. Pass two concrete cairns and cross a bridge over the working railway. At a second bridge Ossian Way is below to your right with the green mound of a covered reservoir beyond it. The bridge has a bright picture painted on it by local school-children.

From here Parkland Walk drops into a cutting between streets. To your right is a steep meadow with silver birches – which would be a good picnic spot if you have brought the makings.

Shortly after the meadow we came across an unusual example of the wildlife the Walk supports. Fred was playing in the undergrowth. A woman stopped to say, 'What a pretty dog' (he receives these undeserved compliments from time to time). Then, 'Is that a petal?' she asked. We both gave him our full attention and realised he was in pursuit of something that moved. I called him off and there, cowering in the nettles, was a tiny, white mouse. The woman picked it up. How could anyone abandon it here, she wondered, where dogs less biddable than Fred would come along? More pressing, I felt, was what to do with the little mite.

'No problem,' she said. 'My neighbour's daughter keeps white mice. She'll be delighted to have another.' She pocketed it and went on.

Pass beneath a sign for the Crouch Hill Recreation Centre and be careful! There are two rinks for skateboarding to your left. If your dog runs across them he is liable to be chopped in two or cause a nasty accident. Fred ran across the first one, luckily without serious mishap. I arrived at the rinks to find a grey-faced teenager, perched on the rim of one of them, muttering, 'Shit!', while Fred bounced eagerly on the surface of the rink, grinning widely at the prospect of a game. So if your dog's inclined to join in when he sees children having boisterous fun, put him on the lead until well past the rinks.

To reach Archway

Directly after the rinks take the path leading upwards to the left. At the top, turn left beside the Recreation Centre. When you reach the building snap on the lead – the fence has gaps. Follow Hill Rise Road to cross Hornsey Road straight ahead by the zebra and Beaumont Road to the left. Enter Elthorne Park and release your dog. This is a poop scoop park. Go straight ahead passing a black sculpture with many faces, then a children's playground. Turn left to cross a grassed area surrounded by trees, so thoroughly surrounded that in summer it's like a green room, with the noise of the nearby traffic muted by the natural sound insulation of leaves and branches. A word here about Islington's policy on dogs in parks. It has a different one for each open space – even those smaller than my back garden – with signs saying where dogs are allowed as well as dog waste bins. There are over 100 of these spaces: surprising, restful places mostly created – and thoughtfully landscaped – within the last decade or so. Speaking of smallness, you will by now have reached the end of your path.

Put your dog on the lead, cross Hazelville Road by the zebra and go straight ahead to enter a housing estate interspersed with walk-ways. Go as straight as you can (the walk-ways will force you to make diversions) to Mount Carmel School: you'll approach it from the back but, with its large tarmac playground, it's obvious that it's a school. Skirt it to the left and go straight ahead again, turn right at Ashbrook Road, cross a tiny green space and go along Geisbach Road. Turn right at Holloway Road to cross its first leg at the lights. Pass a superloo, cross the second leg, turn right and cross Junction Road to Archway station – it has a long stretch of spiral stairs. Archway is where Dick Whittington turned at the sound of the bells – there is a stone cat in an iron cage a short way up Highgate Hill to the east of the station to mark the spot. But this grimy place with the wind whistling round Archway Towers is unlikely, these days, to convince any one London's lure.

To continue on the main route

Once past the rinks, release your dog and look up! Suspended high on an old brick wall is a sculpture, life-sized and apparently flying, of someone who could be an ancient god, could be Pan, could be the mythic Green Man said to fertilise the crops each year. I don't know who he is. There are often climbers below him, festooned with ropes and crampons, preparing to scale the wall. Go under the next bridge and the Walk rises – it is as close to a country bridleway as you are likely to find so near to central London. Keep going until you see, in front of you, two towering brick arches under which the railway used to pass. Follow the gravel path curving left, put your dog on the lead, turn right on Holmesdale Road, right again on Archway Road to cross Shepherd's Hill at the lights. Turn right, then almost immediately, left before the library to release your dog on a wood-land path. Watch out in spring for a wondrous carpet of bluebells to the right of the path behind a paling fence. Very soon descend a flight of rough steps and the path tumbles you out onto Priory

Gardens. Put your dog on the lead, cross the road and turn right to reach, past a row of thirties houses, an elderly signpost. One rusting arm points down a path to the left. On it are the words, 'Footpath. Queen's Wood. Wood Lane. Highgate.' Take the path and release your dog.

Descend the steep slope to murky, bosky Queen's Wood. There are no restrictions on dogs here. At the information board take the left fork and climb the hill. Continue straight, keeping an eye on your dog; there are plenty of squirrels to tempt him to dash across the road ahead. Put him on the lead to cross Queen's Wood Road, then release him again.

It's hard to imagine, but once all London looked like Queen's Wood, a wilderness of tall trees with anemones, celandines and bluebells below. The wood is a remnant of the ancient forest which once covered the London area. As early as the Iron Age people coppiced the trees – cutting them to ground level to provide fuel, then letting them grow again. In the twelfth century the wood still seems to have been fairly large. Wrote William Fitz Stephen, 'Close by the north side of London lies an immense forest in which are densely wooded thickets, the coverts of game, red and fallow deer, boars and wild bulls.' The woods were cleared and replaced first with farmland, then houses. The pockets of trees which survived did so because they provided fuel. In the nineteenth century they passed into public ownership. I'm glad they did. It is hard to do justice to this fragment of forest with its charming, sun-dappled glades and rippling streams into which few people ever seem to venture.

Follow a wide, leaf-mouldy path sloppy right from the road, the next distinct path left, then right. At the bottom of the hill, turn sharp left beside a stagnant pool to reach, after several pleasant minutes, the gate onto Muswell Hill Road. With your dog on the lead cross at the lights and release him in Highgate Wood. Highgate Wood has more people in it and more dogs. Take the concrete path to the left and when it intersects a second path continue straight through the trees. At the sports ground follow a path to its left (little point going to the right of the ground, the cafe there doesn't allow dogs in its garden). I keep a close eye on Fred here, there are always umpteen people playing ball games. He has a thing about balls – he steals them and brings them to me as though I had trained him to do so. In spring there are primroses to the right of the path. At the further end of the ground follow the path as it veers right, stay to the left of cricket slips, take a small path over a stream, join the main path to the right and turn left to reach, in a few moments, Bridge Gate.

To reach Alexandra Park BR, Bowes Park BR, Bounds Green and Wood Green – and for a circular walk to Highgate

Exit at Bridge Gate and turn right on a continuation of Parkland Walk. At Muswell Hill Road put your dog on the lead and turn left down the sloping path under the bridge to regain the Walk and release your dog. A high point of this stretch is the bridge over St. James's Lane from which you can see most of the landmarks you can from viewpoints in subsequent walks – Canary Wharf, Crystal Palace and the black horizon of the Downs beyond. Follow the Walk to Muswell Hill, take the subway under the road and the next path right through a covered walkway which has a mural on it and leads to the open space of The Grove. The Grove contains a very good vegetarian cafe – 'no cappucino, no junk' proclaims the notice outside. In summer there are live shows here. Dogs must be on a lead near the cafe.

Continue on the path, passing a car park to the right, turn right at the next junction and go through shrubs to the road which runs through Alexandra Park. Put your dog on the lead to cross it and walk down the hill to the right on the grass. Keep going until it seems safe to release him, head for a green track which curves downhill, then becomes a footpath. You will join a tarmac path.

Circular walk to Highgate

Cross the wide expanse of grass below the path and follow the line of trees to the right to the access road. On some weekends it's open to traffic; if not your dog can run free. At the ornate gates to the park put him on the lead and slip to the left through the gap. Cross at the lights to reach Park Road straight ahead and walk to the zebra. Cross to the right, cross Cranley Gardens to the left and continue on Park Road past a cricket ground. Take the footpath to your right through a green gate and release your dog. Immediately before Georgian's Club (a tennis club), take the path to your left along an avenue lined with tall trees. There are cricket fields with open gates and more tennis courts, so if your dog chases balls be careful. Turn right at the tarmac track, cross a small car park and – beneath a sign banning motorcycles and cars – release your dog. You are on Woodland Walk, a hidden corner of wild London as charming and as restful as Gillespie Park. Follow the path to the first main fork, go right through woods, cross a meadow, keeping to the right of it and into more woods to pass through an iron gate. Be warned that, although there are wood steps and walk-ways in places, this stretch can be *very* muddy. Turn left on a narrow road and immediately right along a path through woods. Your dog can explore the gullies between trees while you admire the neatly-tended allotments to the left. At the end of the woods, go through another gate and turn left. You are in Queen's Wood at the bottom of the steep path which leads to Priory Gardens. Go up it, put your dog on the lead, turn right and find Highgate tube at the end of the street. It has stairs.

To continue to Alexandra Park BR

Turn left along the path. Alexandra Park has enough attractions for your dog to make an exploration of it quite sufficient for his daily outing. When I can't exercise Fred he comes here with his walker and returns exhausted and covered in mud. The mud is from the south eastern end of the park where the terrain is wildest with streams running through scrub to the west of the Nature Reserve. If you go into the Nature Reserve you must keep your dog on a short lead, none of your fifteen foot extension jobs please. But there's plenty of other space in which your dog can run free.

At the low fence which surrounds the golf course, turn right and follow the path until the road above looks too close for comfort. Strike out to the right until you reach the tarmac path once more, turn left and reach a traffic barrier. Follow the road as it leaves the park, put your dog on the lead and take the footbridge over the railway to the right to find Alexandra Park BR.

To reach Wood Green

For some time you have been following the course of a proposed green trail across Haringey. There is more to come, though none as pleasant as the section you have covered. Cross Buckingham Road, turn right, cross again to Avenue Gardens and release your dog. Follow the path to the right, then cut across the grass to the left. Join another path and stay on it through sad-looking Nightingale Gardens. Cross Bounds Green road with your dog on the lead, turn right along Trinity Road, right on High Road and cross the road at the Civic Centre. Turn right into the ornamental gardens. At the end of the gardens go straight down High Road to find Wood Green station. It has escalators, so you'll have to carry your dog.

To reach Bowes Park BR and Bounds Green

Turn left on Bounds Green Road to find both stations. From Bounds Green if you want to walk along Pymmes Brook (see Walk 14) go straight along Brownlow Road, cross Bowes Road, to take Powys Lane, turn left on Ashridge Gardens and enter Arnos Park. But we'll leave that for another day shall we?

To continue on the main route

Leave Highgate Wood at Bridge Gate to follow a path straight ahead between fenced gardens. At Lanchester Road put your dog on the lead, cross, turn right, cross Woodside Avenue and turn half left down Fordington Road. When the road veers left cross to the right and go left into Cherry Tree Wood. Release your dog and walk along the tarmac path. There is a friendly cafe opposite the tennis courts. Dogs aren't allowed on the cafe forecourt, but Fred doesn't mind. He likes to chase the tennis balls from the wrong side of the wire mesh while I have a cup of coffee. Be careful if your dog likes to do the same – there's a gap in the mesh to the left. From the cafe cross the grass to the right of the courts and take the path beside the railway through woods. At the end of the park East Finchley station (it has stairs) is across the road. Your dog may sleep on the way home. So may you. As for me I've been dreaming of pasta with a glass of red wine these past two miles. Has Fred been dreaming of Pedigree Chum?

I've been dreaming of pasta with a glass of red wine these past two miles. Has Fred been dreaming of Pedigree Chum?

Walk 2: Angel to Camden Town

A stroll along the Regent's Canal, then across the open grassland of Regent's Park and Primrose Hill. Not ideal for dogs who don't like crowds (especially at weekends when Chapel Market and Camden Lock Market are in full swing) but still one of the best outings available this close to the city centre. Connects with Walks 5, 8, 18 and 19.

Route: Angel to Chalk Farm or Primrose Hill BR via King's Cross and Camden Town. Extension Walks to umpteen other places.

Distance: 5 miles

Facilities: Loos in Regent's Park and at King's Cross station. Cafe in Regent's Park. Plenty of pubs, cafes, hot dog, burger, mushy peas etc. stands along the route.

You have several minutes of road walking before the first open space so it is worth mentioning Islington's policy on dog fouling. If your dog's gutter trained, no problem. If not, pick it up. There is another drawback at the outset of this walk; there are no fixed stairs at Angel station, only two very long escalators. This is surprising as the station has recently been refurbished and London Transport has been making quite an effort to make stations accessible to everyone – including the owners of guide dogs. However, you can easily reach the starting point by bus, on which there are no restrictions (subject to the discretion of the bus driver) as long as you and your dog scramble upstairs.

Leave the tube/bus stop. Turn right on Islington High Street, walk to the lights and cross Upper Street to your left. Turn left and cross Liverpool Road – again at the lights. To your left is Chapel Market; to avoid the crowds, go straight up Liverpool Road, turn left into Tolpuddle Street, right along Penton Street to reach Barnsbury Road. Cross Copenhagen Street, enter Barnard Park to the left and release your dog. Barnard Park is one of the few Islington open spaces in which there are no restrictions on dogs. It's described in the coun-

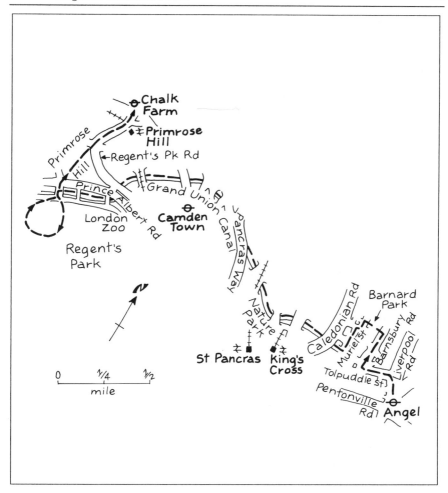

cil's bumf as 'open parkland', but that's much too rural for the small scrap of green it really is. Still, it's big enough for a game of ball. Head straight downhill, cross a redundant road and follow the track made by people's feet. At Hemingford Road put your dog on the lead and turn left. Cross Hemingford Road to your right, Copenhagen Street to your left and go straight along Muriel Street (which is actually a path through a housing estate). Cross Carnegie Street and enter the open gate to the right onto the tow-path beside the Regent's Canal.

Here – if your dog is sensible – he/you can have a great time. There are ducks on the canal, Canada geese and other dogs to meet. Unfortunately, ever since Fred took a step back from the edge of the Exeter Ship Canal, disappeared from sight and had to be hauled out by his collar (I was dripping wet by that time too) I don't trust him near deep water. So he stays on the lead. There are no restrictions on dogs on the tow-path except the usual one of cleaning up.

We have only a short stretch beside the canal on this walk, but it is possible to walk about 40 miles in all along tow-paths right across London from Limehouse Basin in the east to Uxbridge in the west (see Walks 5, 18 and 19).

As you start this walk the Islington Tunnel is behind you. Opened in 1820, it is 960 yards (874m) long and has no towing path – the bargees 'legged' their craft along, lying on top of the boats on their backs and walking upside down on the roof of the tunnel to push the barges through.

To reach King's Cross

At York Way leave the canal path with your dog on the lead and turn left. At the main junction with Euston Road cross by the lights to the right and the station is in front of you.

To continue on the main route

On the opposite side of the water are the gas holders at King's Cross. Shortly after them are the water plants of Camley Street Natural Park – a two-acre (0.8 hectare) nature reserve in the desert of roads and rubbish tips to the north of King's Cross. It was developed by the GLC and is home to birds, butterflies, frogs and toads. But not to dogs. A small site this close to the city centre is too precious for the likes of Fred to be allowed to run loose. Shortly after Camley Street a blue bridge carries the main Intercity railway over the canal. A large, old, iron hulk rots in the water below it. The next bridge carries above it an ad for the Constitution pub, which has a beer garden. Two more bridges, two more locks and you're at the black bridge which signals your arrival at Camden Lock. Pass under it and, if it's the weekend, put your dog on the lead as you're suddenly in the centre of the market with stalls on either side and hordes of people.

There are ducks on the canal. Canada geese and other dogs to meet.

To reach Camden Town

Don't go into the market. Instead cross the arched iron bridge over the canal and turn left along the footpath. Make sure your dog is on the lead when you emerge into Camden High Street and turn right. The street is seriously trendy with cafes (there are sandwich bars etc. from which you can buy a snack without having to go inside); and shops and stalls selling second hand levis, leather jackets, jewellery and tee-shirts. Cross to the left to Camden Town tube. It has stairs. The station is closed for most of the day on Sundays (the busiest day for the market).

To continue on the main route

You've turned right into the market. Keep going as straight as you can with a small inlet of water to your left and some steps to first floor shops to your right. Circle the inlet of water, keeping the buildings of the market to your right to return to the tow-path. If you're lucky there may be an Irish fiddler playing under the next bridge, which is home to the Pirate Club – a canalside youth club built in the 1970s in the image of a medieval castle complete with battlements and drawbridge. A notice warns boaters of a sharp bend to come. Turn it and you are in Cumberland Basin, which is full of narrow boats. You may find an artist with an easel (we did) painting the bright red pagoda (the Gallery Boat Chinese Restaurant) which presides over the basin. Shortly after you will walk between the enclosures of London Zoo.

To reach Greenford and Willesden Junction (see Walks 5 and 18)

Simply keep going along the tow-path across west London. Stations en route are: Warwick Avenue, Paddington (if you sample the Paddington Basin), Westbourne Park, Kensal Green, Willesden Junction, Harlesden and Alperton. There is access to the canal at each one. Beyond Greenford you can continue to Hayes BR, West Drayton BR and Uxbridge. Some stretches of the canal can be quite lonely so British Waterways advise you to take a friend. When I go, I'll take Fred.

To continue on the main route

At the next bridge (Primrose Hill Bridge) exit to the right up the steep path. Cross the bridge to the left, keeping an eye on your dog as the road you are about to cross (The Outer Circle) is wide and cars travel quite fast. Put him on the lead, cross the road and enter Regent's Park. The Park – as most people know – is a Royal Park. It began life as a hunting ground for deer. Henry VIII used to hunt on it. It was laid out in the 1820s by John Nash. All the grass is flat and rigourously mown. However, it is calm and green and – at 102 hectares – delightfully large an open space for central London. It is an ideal place for a ball game, there are is no wildlife (except the ubiquitous grey squirrel) for your dog to disturb. Incidentally, grey squirrels aren't native to Great Britain; they were introduced from north America early this century. Regent's Park was one of the original release sites in which 91 squirrels were set free. Barring a hiccup in the 1930s when they were shot as pests, they have been multiplying ever since.

Retrace your steps and cross Primrose Hill Bridge. Cross Prince Albert Road by the zebra crossing and enter Primrose Hill. This is also open grassland (22 hectares of it) with the fine views across London which distinguish so many open spaces to the north of the river. Take the right fork of the path and continue straight ahead. At the left fork in the path you can climb the summit and look across the West End from 65 metres above sea level. For the shortest route don't turn left but press on to leave the Hill at the gate on the junction of Primrose Hill Road and Regent's Park Road. With your dog on the lead cross Primrose Hill Road and go straight along Regent's Street, passing lots of cafes and bistros which in summer have seats outside. At the junction with Gloucester Road go straight onto the footpath over the railway. Primrose Hill BR is to your right. There is a sign here to Chalk Farm tube. Follow it down Bridge Approach and across Adelaide Road. The station has a lift and/or stairs.

Walk 3: Tottenham Hale to Manor House

A watery walk with a river, ponds, a marsh, and lakes. A walk of contrasts too: from the flat, prosaic landscape of east Hackney to a wooded cemetery which came as a complete surprise. Connects with Walks 1 and 19.

Route: Tottenham Hale to Manor House with diversions to Bromley-by-Bow and Clapton BR.

Distance: 7 miles

Facilities: Loos in Springfield Park, Clissold Park and Finsbury Park. Open air cafes at Lea Valley Marina, Springfield Park and Clissold Park. Pubs with gardens on the river.

Climb the stairs from the platform, follow the signs for Ferry Lane along the subway and when you emerge turn left. At a gap in corrugated iron fencing turn right down a flight of steps and left across a grassy patch. Don't release your dog unless you are confident he will keep away from nearby traffic. Cross Jarrow Road ahead and find the footpath running alongside the river Lea or Lee to your right. You are now in Lee Valley Park. There are no restrictions on dogs in the Park – so if yours is a sensible sort you can let him off the lead. Knowing how daft Fred can be about water and seeing just how deep and wide the river is and how steep its banks, I didn't risk it.

The first thing to know about Lee Valley Park – because it's astounding – is that had you turned north off Ferry Lane you could have walked all the way to Hertfordshire. The Park is 23 miles long and covers 10,000 acres (4,000 hectares). At its central London end, it penetrates the heart of the East End.

Each stretch has a different character – though each is as watery as the one we're covering. There are reservoirs and flooded gravel pits, parkland and farmland and facilities, both formal and informal for just about every sport you can imagine. There is even a camp-site.

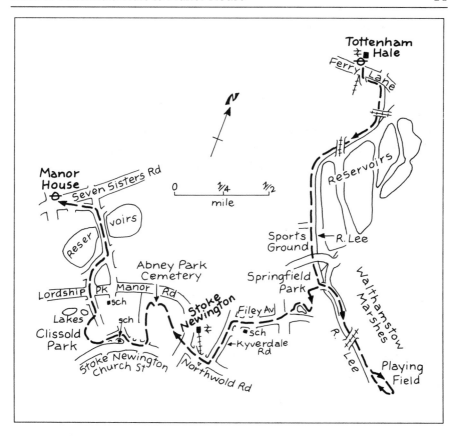

One day I want to walk from end to end of the park, out into the countryside, across peaceful farmlands and water meadows: and return by train.

But not today. Today I have just passed under a railway bridge (the railway is as much a feature of this part of the walk as water is) and have spotted an opening to my right. Step inside and release your dog to follow a footpath running beneath trees alongside the fence between you and the river. You will soon rejoin the river and – Fred being the dog he is – I replaced the lead. There were narrow boats moored on the opposite bank. You will pass, on your right, some sheds filled with skiffs as the tow-path widens into a yard – and find a cafe with tables and chairs outside on the paved ground. Cross the footbridge to the left along a path between notices warning of deep water, then turn right over a bridge under which the water looks very deep indeed. The path becomes a wide, gravel drive (Sandy Lane). Take the drive towards Lea Bridge Road, then stop. To your left is a stile.

This is the entrance to Walthamstow Marshes. As long as you are sure your dog will not dash madly through the undergrowth upsetting all the other animals who live here, then release him. Climb the stile and follow the right fork of the path. Walthamstow Marsh is one of the last surviving examples of marshland in the entire London area. Like many of the so-called marshes in this part of the Park it was once lammas land – land used for common grazing from August till April. But unlike the other marshes, it has remained untouched since the Middle Ages. It covers 88 acres (35 hectares) which, considering it is a mere six miles from Piccadilly Circus, is remarkable. Its success as a wildlife habitat is proved by the story of the Great Crested Grebe. During the last century this odd, colourful creature became almost extinct, such was the demand for its feathers from milliners for ladies' hats. Now about 250 grebes live in the Lee Valley.

Skirt a small, fenced pond to your left across a wooden walkway to emerge in a picnic area. Stay on the path and return to Sandy Lane with the river on your right. I risked leaving Fred off the lead here – and look what happened.

To your left is a swampy ditch. A sign above it explains that the ditch is important to wildlife so please keep your dog out. Fred took one look at ditch and sign and plunged. The water was deeper than he expected; he struggled. A few metres ahead a group of schoolkids and their teacher were examining the glassy surface of the water with meticulous attention.

'I see something blue,' said one child.

'I see a creepy sort of insect,' said another.

Soon they wouldn't see anything if Fred went on wallowing. I hauled him out and instructed him to 'leave' the ditch. One of the rewarding things about walking new terrain with your dog (or so I find) is that you meet new challenges – like the ditch – about which you have to communicate your wishes to him. Making sure that you have made yourself clear and ensuring that he sticks to what you've said is just as valuable – and much more natural – training as the more formal discipline of an obedience class. Not that I've anything against obedience classes. I had a great deal of help with Fred in his early post-Battersea days from Islington Council's Animal Wardens at the weekly sessions they run.

You will come across a board-walk on your left. This takes you out into the fastnesses of the marsh. Fred and I tried it but the prospect of deep undergrowth on either side and the rustling of creatures within was too much for him. A notice pleads that you stick to the board-walk so as not to disturb the wildlife. That was clearly beyond Fred; so we returned to Sandy Lane.

Continue south beside the river. On the opposite bank are several pubs – the Robin Hood, the Anchor and Hope, the King's Head – all of which have gardens. If we'd stayed on the other side we could have stopped at one of them – and followed a different walk: from Springfield Park along the tow-path to the northern corner of North Millfields recreation ground, across that open space and right up Gunton Road to Clapton BR.

After the nature reserve is Leyton Marsh. It was infilled with rubble after the Blitz and is now a dull, flat field. I consulted my A to Z and decided whether to go on. You can go on. You can go across Hackney Marsh which is like Leyton Marsh except that it has hundreds of goal posts for football and rugby. From there cross Homerton Road, Wick Field and the Eastway. Continue along the footpath until you reach the tow-path away to the right along the Hertford Union Canal and follow the tow-path to Victoria Park. (see Walk 19). If you prefer, ignore the Hertford Union Canal, stay on the footpath by the river and continue southwards until you reach the mass of channels known as the Bow Back Rivers. Legend has it that these were created when King Alfred (of burnt cake fame) dammed the river to trap the invading Vikings upstream. Continue on the path, crossing under the railway and over High Street until you reach Three Mill Lane. Turn right and walk between Tesco and a car park. Turn left into Hancock Road and Bromley-by-Bow tube is to the left across the Blackwall Tunnel Northern Approach. It has stairs.

I followed none of these routes. Lee Valley Park publishes ump-teen leaflets which will give you all the information you need on waymarked paths within the Park. But I'm more interested in exploring; so Fred and I retraced our steps.

Back at the cafe outside Springfield Park, release your dog and step inside the park. It's rather typical of Hackney: once the grounds of a country house and now owned by the Borough, it contains a mix of open space; mature trees; flowerbeds; and sports pitches. In case you're wondering, Hackney has no policy on dog mess. They like you to pick it up, there are bins provided for the purpose but there are, as yet, no penalties if you don't.

Ignore the path beside the river and strike straight uphill across the mown grass towards a signpost which points left towards an invisible cafe and toilets. Follow it along a tarmac path to pass tennis courts to your left downhill, then head to the right uphill still on the path. At the summit is a row of seats each with a clipped yew hedge surrounding it as a windbreak. I sat on one to look at the view over the East End while Fred fell asleep under the seat, a tennis ball in his mouth.

Take the path under your feet, which has branched left from the one which brought you up the hill. It leads past a bowling green – a charming reminder of leisurely times past with folk in white outfits playing this slowest of games. The ornamental lake to your right is unsafely fenced: the little loops of wrought iron come up to about knee level, so if you are at all unsure about your dog's behaviour when confronted with throngs of ducks, either stick him on the lead or exit the park by the gate in front of you. If you exit, turn right along Springfield Road.

If you don't exit the park, curve round the lake, keeping it to your left. On your other side is Georgian Springfield House which now houses a cafe and loos. Leave the park by the main entrance, at which point you will join those of us who left earlier. Put your dog on the lead.

Walk along Springfield Road to Upper Clapton Road, turn right and cross by the zebra. Turn left, then right into Filey Avenue. Ignore all turnings to right and left until Filey Avenue comes to an end, turn left into Kyverdale Road and left again at Northwood Road. At a busy intersection with Stoke Newington High Street look ahead –

Fred fell asleep under the seat, a tennis ball in his mouth.

and see the imposing cream-coloured gates of Abney Park Cemetery. Cross the road, enter the cemetery and release your dog.

This place is an enchanting wilderness with tall trees and tumbled tombstones. It's a local nature reserve which the Borough, helped by the Department of the Environment, is restoring. Follow the path straight ahead, then the right fork. On either side are fine displays, on the graves, of urns shrouded in stone fabric; and clasped hands; and crosses with stone ivy trailing up them. There are shady walks too, under tall trees. The cemetery is named for the family of Sir Thomas Abney who held the manor of Stoke Newington in the early eighteenth century. Two centuries later the grounds of his Abney House were amalgamated with those of nearby Fleetwood House and laid out as a burial ground for nonconformists. It proved so popular that soon bodies were crammed into every available space.

Pass the derelict chapel and a large monument. Just beyond a huge, wire litter-basket go left along an established path. Here the tombstones are more elaborate with teenager-sized angels presiding over them. There's a sleeping lion over that of Frank C. Bostock, died 1912. Below the lion is a poem:

On that happy Easter morning
All the graves their dead restore
Father, sister, child and mother
Meet once more

Reach the grave of W. Bramwell Booth, founder of the Salvation Army, to your right. His epitaph glitters in letters of gold. 'Born 8 March 1856. Born of the spirit 1863. Promoted to Glory 16 June 1929.' His wife, Florence E. Booth, is buried in the same grave. Graves of various commissioners of the Army are to the right of the Booths' grave; and to the right of them is a narrow, flagstone path – which you should take. Put your dog on the lead, emerge on Stoke Newington High Street and turn right. A few steps on go right again along a narrow street and when it reaches the main road (Lordship Road), cross and go straight along Lordship Terrace to Clissold Park. Release your dog.

At the rural looking churchyard of St. Mary's turn right into the park, then left with a football area to your right. Clissold Park, like Springfield Park, began life as a private estate attached to a mansion

– Paradise House. The house is on your left, it is built of yellow bricks, dates back to the 1790s and is a listed building. It now houses – you've guessed it – a cafe and loos. In summer there is a mobile snack bar to your right.

The name of the park has a romance behind it. In the early nineteenth century it was the home of banker, William Crawshay. His daughter Elizabeth fell in love with Augustus Clissold, curate at St. Mary's. Crawshay hated parsons. He forbade Augustus to visit the house. The couple sent each other letters; Crawshay threatened to shoot the messengers who carried them. As a last resort he raised the height of the walls around the estate to prevent the lovers catching a glimpse of each other. But Elizabeth and Augustus remained constant. After the old man died, they married, the curate became the new owner of the estate and changed its name to his own.

Keeping the mobile snack bar to your left, strike along the broad concrete path. Take a right at the next fork, towards the right hand end of the ornamental lakes. There are two lakes, side by side, both home to quantities of ducks, but the fences here are high enough to deter your dog unless he is a really accomplished jumper. The lakes aren't natural, they were dug (from the Hackney Brook which now runs underground to the River Lea at Hackney Wick) to provide clay for the bricks to build Paradise House. After Clissold's death the estate reverted to a relative of Crawshay's who put it on the market as a development site. Local people fought for three years to save the park and succeeded when, in 1887, The Metropolitan Board of Works bought the estate. By then the lakes had been filled in. They were immediately re-excavated and named Beckmere and Runtzmere in honour of the two leaders of the campaign.

Had you gone to the other side of Paradise House you would have found a third stretch of water which is a fragment of the New River (see Walk 1). It is worth a visit because of the strange creatures which inhabit it: hundreds of terrapins ranging in size from overlarge buttons to smallish soup plates flop half-in, half-out of the water or sun themselves on the banks. A short walk to the right of the terrapins is an enclosure of deer and ornamental birds. Fred took a particular fancy to a peahen and had to be coaxed away.

After Beckmere and Runtzmere put your dog on the lead at the road (Queen Elizabeth Walk) and turn left. Cross Lordship Park by the zebra to the right. Follow Queen Elizabeth Walk as it veers right and turn left on Lordship Road. Cross between east and west Stoke Newington reservoirs, tell your dog to wait, stop and peer through the fence – you're not allowed in – and see two wide sweeps of water: glimpses of serenity every bit as soothing as our excursion into Abney Park Cemetery. Continue on Lordship Road and, opposite a parade of sad shops, turn left into Woodberry Down and keep straight to reach Manor House tube. It has escalators I'm afraid.

Walk 4: Harrow on the Hill Circular

A cultured walk around the public school with lovely views. The walk's only major drawback is the arterial roads which bisect it. Connects with Walk 5.

Route: Harrow on the Hill Circular Walk, with easy diversions to North-wick Park and South Kenton.

Distance: 3 miles

Facilities: Cafes and pubs in Harrow.

Leave the station by Station Approach, turn right on Lowlands Road, cross it, turn left and cross Landsdowne Road. Strike across the mown grass of the Grove Open Space in front of you (you must pick up after your dog). Release him when you are far enough from the road, cross a tarmac path, then join a path which runs below and to the right of private, fenced woodland. Turn left on Roxborough Road to follow a path which climbs the remainder of the steep hill. At the summit, turn your back on the view (and a viewpoint) to see a tomb in an iron cage. This is the resting place of one John Peachey, but its claim to fame is that Byron used to lie on it to compose his poems – one of them adorns the tomb. A few paces to the left take the tarmac path towards the church. Here I met the owner of Cindy, a black labrador. She pointed out a plaque by the church door in memory of Allegra, Byron's daughter, then invited me to follow her the length of the church, turned left, stopped and showed me a long, low, wooden sign in the undergrowth to the right. On it is inscribed another poem – this time to the memory of Isaac Greentree who planted all the trees around you. Or so said my guide.

Turn right. In a few paces, at Church Hill, put your dog on the lead. Turn right. In another few paces you will see wide, impressive steps to your left on the other side of the lane. Cross and go down them. You are surrounded by the buildings of Harrow School. At the landing in the steps, take the left flight and at the bottom turn

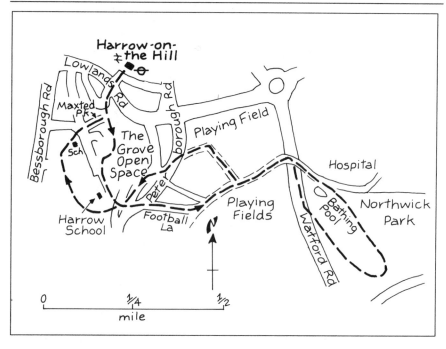

left along High Street. Cross it by the zebra, turn left and follow the
green sign to enter Football Lane and release your dog. Emerge on
playing fields and turn sharp left along the path beside hayfields. If
you look to your right you may see cows grazing on the hill. They
provide milk and butter for the privileged pupils. At Watford Road
put your dog on the lead, cross to Northwick Park Hospital and turn
right to find an entrance to a wooded path on your left. Take it and
release your dog. It soon curves right onto a golf course. I put Fred
on the lead here (because of the golf balls). Strike to the right, step
through a gap in the hedge into Northwick Park and release your
dog.

Northwick Park tube (it has stairs) is a short distance to your left,
South Kenton (also with stairs) a similar distance to your right. We
crossed the park to the right to find a hedgerow and a stream, then
right again into an area of un-mown grass. Cross diagonally (you are
returning to Watford Road and Harrow itself) to a gap in the distant
hedge. Keep going across the wasteland beyond (we saw a Fred-sized
fox here) straight to the fence, turn left and with your dog on the

We saw a Fred-sized fox here

lead slip through a gap in wooden railings and turn right on Watford Road. Shortly, to your right is an extraordinary piece of waste land. Climb over the lumpy ground (you can release your dog) to discover an abandoned swimming pool. It was once the pool for Harrow School and is now called the Ducker Pool.

Retrace your steps to the hospital and cross to take the footpath through the playing fields. Take the first path after the fields to your right. At Peterborough Road put your dog on the lead, turn right, cross the road and go straight up Davison Lane. Go left up Grove Hill, cross it to the right and in a few paces take the opening to the right and climb the steps. Don't release your dog, the path is very short. Cross Church Lane and climb more steps. Release your dog, ascend the steps and you are in the churchyard of St. Mary's. At the viewpoint continue straight down steep steps with the cemetery to your right. At a broad meadow take the right fork in the path and descend across the grass to find a concrete bollard and a path to your right – which you should take. After St. Anselm's church put your dog on the lead, cross Roxborough Park to release your dog and continue on the path to the expanse of grass above Harrow on the Hill station.

Walk 5: Harrow on the Hill to South Greenford

One of the best countryside walks in the capital with acres of meadow-land; woods; hilltop views; lovely picnic spots; and a stroll beside a rural stretch of the Grand Union canal. Connects with Walks 2, 4 and 18.

Route: Harrow on the Hill to Sudbury Hill, Greenford, Perivale and South Greenford BR. An extension walk to Boston Manor is suggested.

Distance: 5 miles

Facilities: No loos – except in pubs along the route.

A warning: if you go in late summer and your dog is long-haired, be prepared to spend the evening picking burrs from his coat.

Start as for Walk 5 and go up the grassy slope beside Landsdowne Road. When you reach the tarmac path at right angles, turn right and follow the path. At Roxborough Road put your dog on the lead, cross, release him, pass St. Anselm's, enter the meadow and follow the lower path which curves right to join Bessborough Road. With your dog on the lead again, turn left, cross West Street, pass cricket grounds and turn left on Middle Path – which is short so keep your dog on the lead. Turn left up Middle Road and next right into Byron Road, then right along West Hill. At Roxteth Hill turn left, cross London Road to your left and follow it round to the right. Cross the road at the next traffic island and walk along the grass. At South Hill Avenue, to your right, follow the signpost down a Green Lane and release your dog. This is a bridleway running through woodland. At South Vale put your dog on the lead, cross and turn left. At the main road (Greenford Road) turn right. Pass Sudbury Hill Harrow BR on your right, cross Greenford Road by the pedestrian crossing and turn right again. You have reached Sudbury Hill tube. It has stairs.

A few steps after it turn left along a cul de sac. It becomes a path on which you can release your dog. Follow the path as it bends right across a green space. At Ridding Lane put your dog on the lead, turn

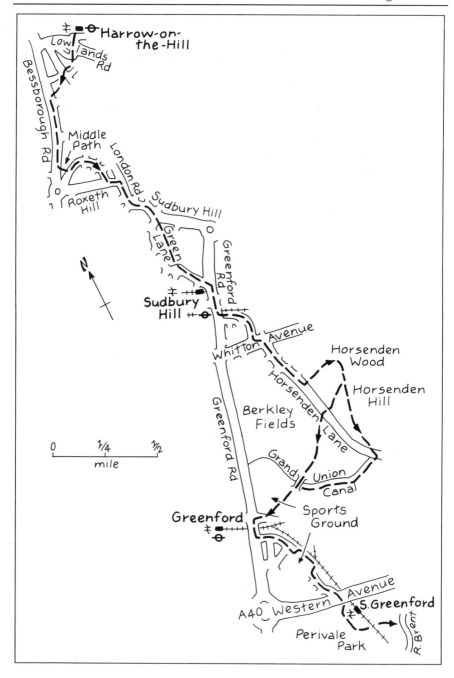

Be prepared to spend the evening picking burrs from his coat.

right and follow the lane to Whitton Avenue East. Cross it by the pelican to your right, turn left and take the next right (Melville Avenue).

Soon Melville Lane becomes Horsenden Lane North; and London becomes a country wilderness. Step onto the footpath to your left just before the Ballot Box pub and set your dog loose. You are at the northern end of Horsenden Hill, 250-odd acres (100 hectares) of glorious open space managed 'for the conservation of wildlife and the enjoyment of the public' by the London Borough of Ealing. Ealing is one of the few London boroughs to have a positive attitude towards dogs. Dogs and their owners are welcome visitors in the borough's parks – all they ask is that you observe the country code.

You are in Ridding Wood – but the open space of New Ballot Box Field, glimpsed through a gap in the hedgerow to the right, proved more enticing. We slipped through the gap into the tall grass of the meadow where butterflies dipped between the seed heads. Turn left along the rough path and go through a thin belt of trees into Horsenden Wood Field. At the end of it is Horsenden Wood – it's a 10 acre (4 hectare) fragment (mainly oak and hornbeam) of London's ancient wildwood. Take the rough path through it to the right. Go straight on up the hill and emerge from the wood with a golf course to your left at the top of Horsenden Hill which is 276 feet (84m) above sea level. You can see the spire of the church at the summit of Harrow's hill. You can see mile upon mile of red rooftops. You can even see the countryside beyond London. Stone Age people though it a good spot too – they settled here 7,000 years ago.

Go straight ahead over a small precipice. You now have a choice of two routes to Greenford tube, both of which entail crossing only one road.

Route 1

Turn left on the grassy plateau below the summit and follow the waymarked path through a gap in the blackthorn hedge to emerge in Home Meadow, a hayfield running downhill. Two men were roaming through the long grass, a third was lolling on the ground, bare-chested and smoking a joint, a fourth was gazing at the view. I think this must be a gay area. Drop down between Home Mead and

London Mead to find a small triangle of wild flowers to the right, just before the path hits Horsenden Lane. Red poppies, blue cornflowers, a profusion of yellow and white daisies – the flowers of traditional English meadows which you are unlikely to come across in the pesticide-drenched fields of the real countryside. The flowers aren't here by chance. The council rotovates the spot annually and scatters the seeds.

To your left is an information board. When we were there, pinned to it was a leaflet detailing events on the Hill. Some of them – all credit to Ealing – are highly imaginative. You can go foraging for fungi each year under the direction of an expert, join a creepy, crawly hunt, explore a bat cave (Yeugh!), watch migrant birds at dawn, or paint and draw from the natural landscape. Most of the events are free, but I daresay some of them are unsuitable for dogs. To find out more, write to: Parks Administration, Leisure Services Division, Perceval House, 14-16 Uxbridge Road, London W5 2HL.

Time to put your dog on the lead. Turn left on Horsenden Lane, pass the entrance to Horsenden Farm and just before the white, hump-back bridge over the canal, take a footway to the left. You will rejoin the road on the other side of the canal and, a few steps further, find the entrance, also to the left, to the canalside path.

If you want to go home, don't take the path but go straight down Horsenden Lane to nearby Perivale tube – which has stairs.

To continue, turn left on the canal path. I kept Fred on the lead here. The water is fringed by greenery – meadows and trees – and you can easily imagine yourself in the countryside. Pass under the bridge. To your left is an open space, then the Perivale Wood Bird Sanctuary which is securely fenced against the likes of Fred. But there are plenty of waterfowl to look at on the canal. On the opposite bank people were fishing and reading *The Sun*. One couple were into some serious necking. Well why not? – the canal is a charming setting for amorous dalliance. Pass under a footbridge, go through a kissing gate to your left and turn right.

Route 2

At this point the followers of Route 2 will join us. From the summit of Horsenden Hill they turned right, reached a gravel path with trail posts and dropped down to the car park. They turned left with their dogs on leads. Just before Horsenden Lane take a few steps to the right and see trail posts to your left onto Horsenden Lane. Cross the road – carefully, the visibility isn't good. Release your dog but keep him close – Ealing Council ask that you stay on the footpath to avoid disturbing birds.

Ivy spreads on either side. You have to bend low to duck beneath half-fallen trees arching across the path. You are in Rohais Wood. It is the overgrown garden of a house called 'Rohais' which was demolished in the 1940s. Follow the path as it swirls to the right and you will find a flight of stone steps leading up on your left to ... nowhere. Once upon a time there were lawns, a rose garden, a rockery, ponds with waterfalls, a fountain, orchards and vegetable plots. Now there is sycamore, oak, wild plum, elm, brambles; a leafy, earthy, green, refreshing scent; and the charm of a secluded woodland path which is hardly diminished by the noise of traffic on Horsenden Lane.

Leave Rohais Wood at a trail post to your right with a wooden seat to the left of it. Turn left along the wide path, then almost immediately right along a trodden path through more meadows. This area has produced hay for many years past. The hay used to be carried into the centre of London on the canal narrow boats to feed the city's carriage horses. The boats would return laden with 'mack' – a fertiliser for the fields made of butcher's waste and horse manure. Nowadays the fields are mown after the grass has seeded, just as they used to be.

Continue across the meadow – it's called Great Bramstones – and follow the waymarked path into Rockware Field. Most of the fields on Horsenden Hill are now known by the names which appeared on a 1773 map of the Parish of Greenford. Once in Rockware Field, take the mown path to the right of a rugby pitch, then turn left at the hedgerow. When you reach a gap in the hedge to the right, exit the field, turn left along a footpath, cross the footbridge over the canal and join the walkers on Route 1.

The path you are now following is a delectable waterside track, rich with bog-loving plants. On the left are tall, brown bullrushes.

On the right is a profusion of blue flowers. I think it's here that Fred caught his crop of burrs.

You'll emerge at the junction of Rockware Avenue and Greenford Road. If you've had enough of walking, cross Greenford Road, persist up Rockware Avenue, turn left at Old Field Lane and catch the tube home from Greenford. The station has stairs.

But we're going on. Turn left and cross Rockware Avenue. Walk along Greenford Road under the railway bridge. It's a shock to find yourself in a busy, metropolitan environment after so much peace. Take the next left (Bennett's Avenue), enter a playing field ahead, turn sharp left and follow the fenced path. Go the length of the playing field to exit the path on Cayton Road and put your dog on the lead. At Runnymede Gardens, a travesty of a road running alongside horrible Western Avenue, turn left and climb the foot-bridge. This scared me stiff – I don't like heights – but Fred thought it was a breeze. Descend the footbridge and you are at journey's end and can catch the train from South Greenford BR to your left. But I didn't; I went a little further to find a perfect picnic place.

After the bridge turn right, then, at the sign to Perivale Park, left into the park – which is flat and characterless. Skirt the running track, keeping it to your left, turn left through a car park, go under the railway bridge to find a wide, green expanse with the charming River Brent meandering behind dense foliage to the left. But what foliage! Cow parsley lookalikes six feet tall. In fact they're giant hogweed, and you shouldn't touch them, they can cause severe skin irritation. I picknicked here while Fred rushed madly about and emerged from the river black from head to paw.

From here you can embark on several lovely walks in the Brent River Park. You can follow the river as it runs south and west, then, when you reach Ruislip Road, circle back to Greenford through Perivale Park. Instead of circling back you can pursue the river beyond Ruislip Road, visit St. Mary 's church which was one of Gilbert Scott's earliest designs and Brent Park Lodge. The Lodge is known locally as the Bunny Park because of the domestic animals kept there in a small zoo. South again, the river leads you past the site of the old Hanwell asylum – a remarkably enlightened nine-teenth century institution whose inmates grew the hospital's vege-tables and baked its bread. It leads you too to the Grand Union Canal and the Hanwell Flight – six locks which raise the water level 53 feet (16m) in a third of a mile. A narrow boat takes about one and a half hours to negotiate them. Continue from there and you'll go past Osterley Island. You could take the track at the far end of the island, to the left, come out on Wyke Gardens, turn right, right again along Southdown Avenue, left into Wellmeadow Road, right on Boston Road and find Boston Manor tube. The station has stairs. From the southern tip of the Brent River Park Osterley Park is within easy reach.

I read about these alluring walks in a leaflet produced by the Brent River and Canal Society and wished I had the energy to tackle them. Instead, after I'd eaten we retraced our steps to South Greenford BR and went home.

Walk 6: Tufnell Park to Golders Green

Across Hampstead Heath with views over the city from Parliament Hill Fields, shallow water if your dog likes swimming and miles of freedom for him in lovely terrain. Connects with Walks 1 and 7.

Route: Tufnell Park or Archway to Golders Green with diversions to Gospel Oak BR and Hampstead.

Distance: 3½ miles

Facilities: Loos on Hampstead Heath. Open air cafes in Waterlow Park, Swains Lane and on Hampstead Heath. Pubs along the route.

From Tufnell Park tube

The station has a lift and stairs. Turn right, cross Tufnell Park Road and go along Junction Road. At Monnery Road cross the zebra to the left over Junction Road and go up Poynings Road. Pass a housing estate and go through a wooden gate on the right to enter Dartmouth Park Hill. There are bins for dog waste in the park, but no one seems to use them so watch where you put your feet. The park is small and relatively featureless. Its attraction is in the steepness of the hill on which it lies and the extensive panorama of the city from the viewpoint at the top of it. Follow the tarmac path to pass a children's play area and sharp left to reach Dartmouth Park Hill (the road). Put your dog on the lead, cross and go straight ahead into Chester Road. Just before the bus stop take a footpath to your left. There are umpteen signs warning you of the penalty (£20) for dog fouling – but the path is still a mess. It isn't securely fenced and there are often cats in the back gardens on either side. At Croftdown Road turn right, left into St. Alban's Road, right along Brookfield Park and left into Swain's Lane.

From Archway tube

Archway station has a long spiral staircase. Leave the tube by the Junction Road exit. Turn right, then right again into litter-strewn

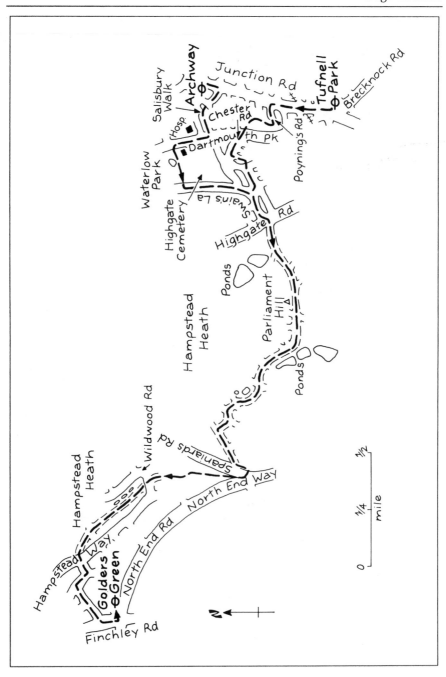

Vorley Road. If your dog is gutter-trained, persuade him to relieve himself here. At the bus depot cross Vorley Road to the left and go through the red gate to the path beyond (Girdlestone Walk). Don't let your dog foul the grass and don't let him run free; there are bye-laws against both since this is the communal garden of a housing estate.

Walk straight past the grass to emerge on Dartmouth Park Hill by a church. There is a pub with a garden to the left. Turn right. You are now in Camden which has the same policy on dog mess as Islington – yellow paintings of squatting dogs on the pavement and yellow arrows pointing to the gutter remind you of this.

Cross Magdala Avenue, climb the hill, then cross to the left to enter Waterlow Park and release your dog. Press straight ahead along the tarmac path.

Alternatively, if you want to explore Waterlow Park you will find it an attractive, hilly place with three ponds (your dog can swim in the dirty top one). It covers 11 hectares and is very popular with chatty local dog owners. It was given to the London County Council in 1889 by Sir Sydney Waterlow as a 'garden for the gardenless'. That was a lovely thought and the park thoroughly lives up to it; formal gardens and a play area at the eastern side soon give way to green glades, then a big grassy expanse and woodland paths harbouring squirrels. The Lauderdale House Cafe (half way up the eastern edge of the park) serves excellent food and permits your dog to sit beside you while you eat at a table on the patio outside.

At Swains Lane Gate put your dog on the lead. The formal part of Highgate Cemetery is across the road. The wilder section in which Karl Marx and George Eliot are buried is to your left. Dogs aren't welcome in either. Cross Swains Lane, turn left and follow the road as it curves right. Pass Brookfield Park and join the walkers who followed the route from Tufnell Park. Cross Swains Lane to reach a pub with a small garden and cross Highgate West Hill by the zebra next to the bus depot to enter Hampstead Heath. And yes, of course your dog can run free. For hours. Do pick up after him, though, especially in the heavily-used areas (this is one of them). There are plenty of dog mess bins at all the entrances to the Heath, most of them surrounded by the evidence of the failure of some owners to bring their plastic bags. Go straight along the tarmac path, then right to the shore of the lowest of the Highgate ponds. Local people call

this the dog pond and come from all over to throw sticks or balls
into the water for their dogs to retrieve. Further out waterfowl perch
on artificial islands. I've seen a pair of herons there and a Great
Crested Grebe.

To reach Gospel Oak BR

Turn away from the pond to the tarmac path. At weekends it is very
crowded. Watch out for roller skaters and cyclists! Turn left. Go
down the gentle hill to the children's play area on your left and a
drinking fountain at the junction of the paths. Loos are in front of
you and there's a cafe to your right. Turn right beyond the cafe, take
the next left alongside William Ellis School to reach Gordon House
Road with the station just to your right.

To continue on the main route

Hampstead Heath is my local park, where Fred and I walk every
morning. Its delights for both dog and owner are endless, whatever
the season. In winter, in deep woods, you can follow the tracks of
rabbits through virgin snow. In spring there are clumps of snowdrops in the enclosed area beside Millfield Lane and the willows
which fringe the Highgate Ponds are tinged with the yellow which
is the first sign of new growth. On a summer Saturday afternoon you
can sit on the hill above Kenwood and listen to an orchestra
rehearsing for the evening's concert. And in autumn the colours of
the turning trees are a delight. Most mornings, rain or shine, a
bagpiper plays on the hills towards Kenwood; he's been playing
there on and off for fourteen years.

On Parliament Hill (otherwise known as Kite Hill) there are, of
course, kites. Turn right from the pond to climb towards the summit.
At the next junction take the right fork. A wide sweep of meadow
spreads away to your right. It's perfect for one of Fred's special
pleasures – tearing round in circles in long grass for no reason at all.
At the top you can enjoy a panoramic view over London. If it's a
weekend Parliament Hill will be crowded – with kite flyers, couples
sunbathing, families having picnics.

Stick to the same path straight ahead to descend the hill. At the
second crossroads carry on straight. The path will curve to the right,

kite flyers, couples sunbathing, families having picnics.

then to the left and you will see Hampstead ponds through the trees to your left.

To reach Hampstead

Go between the ponds and along the path straight ahead. Put your dog on the lead as you approach Heath Road. Cross, release your dog and take the footpath over rough grass ahead. Stumble down the steepish hill. Be sure to put your dog on the lead well before Willow Road as it can be busy. Turn right then left along Gayton Road, right along Hampstead High Street and find Hampstead tube. It has a lift and stairs.

To continue on the main route

Just before the ponds take a sharp right along a dirt track. There's a paling fence on the left, woods on the right. Keep the Mixed Bathing Pond to your left, climb the natural steps formed by tree roots to the right and follow the path through woods. Emerge onto a patch of green. Take the lower path here. Stay on it as it crosses another grassy area, then goes through more trees. Not many people use this path – it's wild, fringed by nettles and docks and feels much more countrified than the stretch of the Heath we have so far crossed. At the next main path go left, then right in a couple of metres. You can see an iron rail to your left, ahead. This, you will soon discover, guards the further bank of a small stream. It's the lost river Fleet after which Fleet Street is named and it's the only stretch of the river which now runs above ground. Beyond the Fleet is Viaduct Pond. Keep it to your right and head uphill to enter a grove of oaks. To your right is a tall tree which looks, as you approach it, like some crouching, mythical beast with an extremely long neck. It's an oak and it's hollow. Most weekends there are kids peering into its belly. At the next main path turn left past loos and a drinking fountain with a bowl around the bottom for dogs to drink from. Turn left along a broad gravel drive to reach Spaniards Road. Put your dog on the lead and cross the road by the zebra. Turn right past the bus stop and onto the narrow path beside the road. In a few metres a path leads into the woods to your left. Take it and release your dog.

You are on Sandy Heath. There are far fewer people and far more mountain bikers than on the Heath proper; and the terrain is a complete change. There are no concrete paths, only scrappy, muddy ones which look as though they've been made by rabbits. If you watch out you may see the rabbits. Follow the right fork (in summer there are wonderful stands of rosebay willow herb and the occasional orchid). The path will lead you between gorse bushes, aflame with yellow blooms. Watch your dog doesn't take a plunge into the small, slime-covered pond beyond. Pass two more ponds and turn right along a substantial path. Turn left, almost immediately, along a rudimentary path which leads downhill. Take the next wide, clear path left, then go right on a smaller path. Put your dog on the lead (watch out, it can be very muddy here), cross Wildwood Road, release him and follow the path ahead beside sloping water meadows.

If you've emerged from the woods at the wrong point, then look for a large, fallen tree, keep it on your left and you will rejoin us. Aim for a smallish, stone monument ahead. It has 'IN MEMORY OF WALTER FIELD ARWS' embossed in stone capitals on its side. Go along the main path. Pass loos and cross the horse ride. You are on a playing field and should take the path which leads half left. Be careful now if your dog is like Fred. People are playing with balls like billy-o. I managed to keep Fred away from the cricketers by offering him a glimpse of the tennis ball I always keep in my pocket; but I hadn't noticed the family game going on the other side of the path. Before I could say, 'Leave,' Fred pounced on their plastic ball and sank his teeth in it. 'Oh dear,' said a sad voice. 'The dog's popped it.'

He had too. I offered to pay for the ball but the nice family said it didn't matter. With Fred now in his halti, we pressed on.

Cross Hampstead Way, go down Corringham Road, take the second left (Rotherwick Road), turn left on Finchley Road and right onto North End Road. The entrance to Golders Green tube (it has stairs) is along a footpath to the left. In fact it's in the bus station.

Walk 7: East Finchley to High Barnet

This is a walk beside the North Circular – but don't be put off. On your other side is a river – albeit a rather eerie one. There is very little road walking, but you are never far from people; and a diversion takes you to an open air theatre in a wood and the mock countryside of Hampstead Garden Suburb. At the northern end of the walk you have three further circular walks to choose from, each of which is a minimum of 5 miles. Best come back another day for these, don't you think? Connects with Walks 1, 6, 14 and 17.

Route: East Finchley to Finchley Central, Brent Cross, Golders Green: or Mill Hill East, West Finchley, Woodside Park, Totteridge and Whetstone or High Barnet.

Distance: 7½ miles (to Woodside Park)

Facilities: Loos in Northway Gardens. Pubs along the route.

East Finchley station has stairs. Exit by the main entrance, turn right past the Old Lion pub (which has a dismal garden at the front of it) and right again along a path (The Causeway) with a cycleway sign above it. The path runs between secure fences, so your dog can run free if he is the quiet sort. Take the next path left, emerge in Edmunds Walk, put your dog on the lead, cross Deansway and follow a narrow path between hedges which crosses Harford Walk and Devon Rise and fetches up in the quiet cul-de-sac of Totnes Walk. Turn left. At Vivian Way turn right, cross major Lyttleton Road and turn right past a mansion block called Monarch Court to take a path to the left. Release your dog. Take the right fork and you are walking alongside Mutton Brook. It is a tributary of the Brent (see Walk 5), but has little of its charm. It is confined by rigid 'banks' of stone and wood. Notices warn that its waters are polluted, so I wouldn't let your dog drink them.

This is a poop scoop park. Cross a small, steep, wooden, humpbacked bridge over the stream to your left to enter a flat open space.

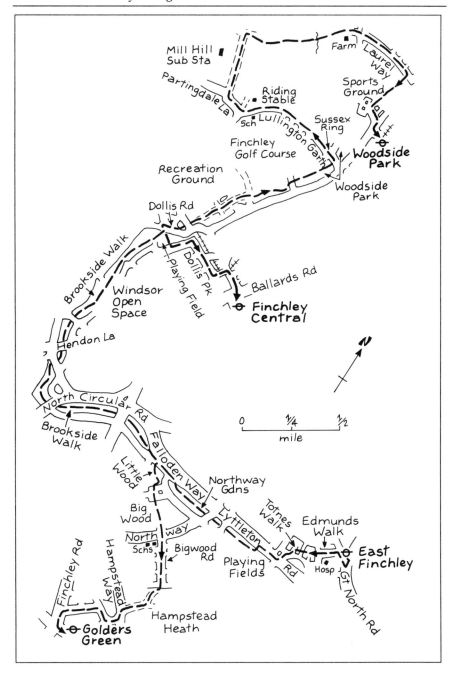

Follow the river and cross Kingsley Way with your dog on the lead. Turn right and rejoin the path. Release your dog. Cross Northway – again with your dog on the lead – to Northway Gardens which have a putting green and tennis courts. Pass pretty Northway Cottage to go through a fine glade of horse chestnut trees. At Falloden Way put your dog on the lead, turn left and left again in Addison Way.

To reach Golders Green

Look for a path waymarked with a green arrow a few metres further to the left along Addison Way. Release your dog and take the path. You are in magical Little Wood with the circular space of the Hampstead Garden Suburb open air theatre to your right. In the past it was used for pageants and it's still the venue for a play presented every midsummer by the local dramatic society. Continue along the tarmac path which skirts the left of the theatre. At the end of the wood put your dog on the lead. You are in Hampstead Garden Suburb – an extraordinary blend of the urban and the rural – with the emphasis on the latter. Every house has a neatly clipped hedge and an immaculate garden. On a weekday the streets are deserted (everyone must be at work) and you can enjoy the lush lawns and bright, herbaceous borders in splendid solitude.

Dame Henrietta Barnett founded the Suburb in 1907. Her idea was that the working classes would benefit from mixing with people from more privileged backgrounds. So terraced cottages and flats were built alongside more substantial houses. The whole was planned by Sir Raymond Unwin with contributions from many leading architects, including Sir Edward Lutyens. These days even the flats would be far beyond the means of any but the very well-off.

Follow Denham Drive North for a couple of minutes to find the footpath through Big Wood in front of you. Release your dog and let him enjoy running through the trees. At a fork follow the waymark to the right. As you leave Big Wood put your dog on the lead and cross North Way into Big Wood Road. Cross Middle Way and look out for topiary on the left. And look under your feet! At the base of a street tree is a plaque which reads: 'Remembering Jack Bamford who loved this spot'. Ignore the streets which cross Big Wood Road at as exact right angles as streets in an American city's grid system.

After a few minutes you will see an opening and green fields beyond. Wait till you reach the opening to release your dog – there are equally inviting driveways to private houses on either side. Step through the opening and find yourself on the northern reaches of the Hampstead Heath extension. Turn right along the footpath, then left across the grass – to find Golders Green tube as per walk 6.

To continue on the main route

Go along Addison Way to take, to the right, a path between houses and release your dog. If it's late summer, there'll be windfall apples on the grass and plump, purple elderberries hanging over it. The path curves to the left into a pretty open space. Cross the brook by the next footbridge to the right. Before the *next* footbridge (to the left of you) turn right, following the path, put your dog on the lead and climb the gentle incline to Finchley Road. Cross it by the lights to the right, turn left and rejoin the path. Be prepared for clouds of midges. Cross a wide meadow, press on across a tiny bridge over a tiny stream and go under a white, arched bridge – I kept Fred on the lead for the duration on account of the depth of the water – over which the North Circular runs. When we were there a shopping trolley languished in the water (from nearby Brent Cross I assume). After the bridge your dog has a meadow in which to run. At the next bridge, follow the path away from the river to the right, then left behind the backs of houses in Southborne Crescent. The tarmac path curves to the left. There is a post with a green arrow on it to confirm that you are headed in the right direction.

You have now left Mutton Brook for Dollis Brook which is a second tributary of the Brent. The Brent itself runs south through Brent Park to Brent Street. From there it is a short, not particularly attractive walk to Brent Cross tube.

If you stay on the banks of the Dollis you reach a path leading right at the end of the houses. It is worth stopping to inspect the board to your right which gives information about the Dollis Greenway. The Greenway is another of London's linear parks, a green corridor 10 miles long which connects Hampstead Heath with Scratchwood Country Park and Moat Mount open space. Both of these are huge tracts of countryside well worth a day's visit. The word is that they support breeding populations of muntjacs (see page 6). From Scratchwood it is a feasible – through extremely lengthy – project to trek across country to Stanmore where there are lovely walks. Stanmore isn't accessible by public transport, so I went there by car, with a friend. I recommend you do the same one summer afternoon if you can arrange it. From the car park and picnic area on Old Redding Road (which has superb views over the city) turn right past a pub called The Case is Altered – the name is a corruption of 'Casa Alta' or 'high house', so called because from its garden you can see six counties. After the pub cross the road and turn right through woods so green and deep you almost expect to see Robin Hood thundering towards you on a white stallion. The walk is a circular one and crosses the thickety wilderness of Bentley Priory Open Space. Watch out for long-horned cows – Fred was fascinated by them, I thought I wouldn't want to get on the wrong end of them. Watch out too for cow pats, in which your dog might roll – Fred did. As the walk turns south you cross a lush deer park (in which the deer are protected from your dog by secure fences). On the last leg of the walk there are riding stables and country lanes. A longer walk in the area passes by Grim's Ditch, an ancient Saxon earthwork which runs for three miles between Harrow Weald Common and Pinner Green. For more information on these walks, contact: London Borough of Harrow, Parks Service, Civic Centre, Harrow, HA3 5BD.

And what a long way I've strayed from our original walk. If you're still on it pass under another bridge – North Way runs over it – into denser woodland and long grass. The river forks around a tiny, wooded island. Beyond the island is a waterfall. Put your dog on the lead and go through the (lit) subway under Hendon Lane. Follow the path to the right of the brook. There are no red notices proclaiming that the Dollis is polluted and it certainly looks a lot cleaner than Mutton Brook. Some of its banks are bulwarked by stone or planks, but there are stretches now where it flows in natural meanders and there are small 'beaches' onto which your dog can scramble. I let Fred do so, let him drink the water and he suffered no ill effects.

Cross Waverley Grove with your dog on the lead and continue through Windsor Open Space. Stay beside the brook – it's a tidy way – until you reach a dead end with a fence of silver metal palings in front of you.

To reach Finchley Central

Turn right along the securely fenced path. At Lyndhurst Road put your dog on the lead, turn left, then right on Dollis Hill. Pass Crescent Road to your left, and – opposite another Crescent Road to your right – turn left along the footpath. Cross the railway by the blue bridge. On the other side a Russian vine runs riot, Turn right into Nether Street, right into Ballards Lane, cross the next pedestrian crossing and turn left. Walk back up the main road, turn right into Station Road and find Finchley Central. It has stairs.

To continue on the main route

Turn left at the fence. Put your dog on the lead to emerge at the junction of Thornfield Avenue and Dollis Road. Turn right and pass under the soaring red brick arches of the Mill Hill viaduct. It was built in the early 1860s for the Great Northern Railway branch to Edgware and now carries London Underground trains on the Northern line to Mill Hill East.

As the road bends sharply to the right, cross it to the left (carefully, there is a great deal of traffic), go down the waymarked path opposite and release your dog. You are in woods, through which the Dollis wanders. To your left is Finchley Golf Course. I was thinking about eating my picnic, but all of a sudden I came to a path which crossed ours at right angles. Our own path stopped. Had I consulted my leaflet on circular walks around Totteridge and Mill Hill I would have realised that I had reached the southern end of the red walk and could have turned left along Lovers Walk for a circuit of the Totteridge Valley.

But I'm glad I didn't do that. What I did instead was to combine bits of the red walk and the yellow walk. You won't know what I'm talking about, quoting colours at you, so I'll explain. Barnet Council, as well as publishing a leaflet on the Dollis Greenway, has one on each of three circular walks: the blue walk, the yellow walk and the red walk. The blue walk sounds particularly enticing (perhaps because it's the one we didn't do?). It goes round Mill Hill village and along a disused Underground line.

If you turned left along Lovers Walk, then right at Frith Lane, took the next left, third left again into Drew Avenue which becomes Bray

Road, turned left on the Ridgeway, then right into Sanders Lane, you could join the blue walk. It'll be waymarked with blue arrows as the two walks I chose are with red and yellow ones. The blue walk is 5 miles and crosses Bittacy Park, acres of open space around Folly Brook (which flows into the Dollis), Totteridge Common, Arandene Open Space and Featherstone Hill. The two last are 25 hectares of grassland designated as meadows of metropolitan significance by the London Ecology Unit. They have rolling fields separated by streams and mature hedges. On the highest point of Featherstone Hill, you can look down to the south on the valley of the Silk Stream.

As for me and Fred we're a couple of pages of the A to Z behind you, dithering on the Dollis Brook at the junction with Lovers Walk. We turned right and crossed the bridge.

To reach West Finchley

Put your dog on the lead to cross Brent Way and continue on Lovers Walk to Nether Street. Turn left and follow the street to find the station. It has fixed stairs.

To continue on the main route

Turn left after the bridge and cross Fursby Avenue with your dog on the lead to return to the linear park. I released Fred. We were in an open space with tennis courts ahead and I was starving. I didn't trust Fred near tennis balls, so I crossed the stream by the bridge to the right, found a shady spot and collapsed on the grass. We shared a sandwich of garlic and brandy pate and tomato. I checked my maps and realised I could sample the yellow walk if we pressed on a little further to the north.

If you don't want to do this, continue following the red waymarks until you reach Totteridge Lane, turn right and find Totteridge and Whetstone station. It has stairs.

To find the yellow route

We crossed back over the bridge to the left, then turned right past the tennis courts. Soon we hit Sussex Ring (that's a road). The red walk leads straight ahead. I turned left and found we faced quite a bit of road walking. At the roundabout press straight on into Lull-

We shared a sandwich of garlic and brandy pate.

ington Garth. The road will tilt left and there will be a stile to your right with a signpost indicating a footpath. Don't follow it – it leads through a field of horses and it is an offence under the Wildlife and Countryside Act of 1981 for a dog to be at large in a field where there is livestock unless the dog is on a lead or otherwise under close control.

At the main entrance to the Equestrian Centre turn right along Partingdale Lane. At the next curve, Burtonhole Lane leads to the right and you should follow it. It's been called Burtonhole Lane for over 200 years. There was a fifteenth century tenant farmer hereabouts called Robert Burton. Hole probably means hollow. These days the lane is a bridleway. On either side are fields of horses, insecurely fenced.

At a stile to the left, follow the sign pointing along a footpath to Totteridge. There were no horses in the pastures so I let Fred loose. I climbed the slow incline to find that he had wriggled through a gap in the fence and was eyeball to eyeball with a big, black gelding. I whistled him and – phew! – he came away.

To your right are views of London. Continue along the path as it dips to the right and cross a barrier to ascend the hill. Climb a stile and put your dog on the lead – quick as you can. To your right are more horses and between you and them is an electric fence. An electric fence is a pretty nasty experience for a horse, it would be a horrible one for your dog.

Climb the stile at the top and follow a narrow path behind houses to emerge on a delightful village green. Turn right and in a few steps there is a charming scene of white houses clustered round a duck pond. Ahead, slightly to the left, go through the gateway with a path visible beyond to turn left into Laurel Way – and return, in a stride, to suburbia, albeit the well-heeled sort. Continue on Laurel Way, cross Northiam and the Dollis riverside walk is to your right.

If you want you can follow the red walk north and circle Brook Farm Open Space, through King George's Playing Fields to Moat Mount Open Space and thence to Scratchwood Open Space. You can return via Totteridge Park Open Space, and Totteridge Common to Burtonhole Lane. If you press on further north you can find High

Barnet tube and come home from there (see Walk 14 on how to make the connection).

But we turned south along the riverside walk. At Tillingham Way turn left, then right at Holden Road. Woodside Park tube is on the opposite side of the road up the incline of Station Approach. It's painted green and cream, has flowers on the platform and seems a world away from London; but in a few minutes we were home.

Not many other dogs (except toys), few friendly dog owners.

Walk 8: Embankment to Lancaster Gate

The Royal parks and the Serpentine.

Route: Embankment to Notting Hill Gate or Queensway via Westminster, St James's Park, Green Park, Hyde Park Corner, Marble Arch and Lancaster Gate.

Distance: 4 miles

Facilities: Loads of them, pretty much everywhere.

You can work out this walk for yourself by looking at the A to Z, you don't need me to do it for you. St James's Park is full of birds. Fred and I tried Green Park and Hyde Park and didn't like them much either. Not many other dogs (except toys), few friendly dog owners; and people took a dim view of Fred chasing squirrels. The parks are too formal, too unsurprising for my taste. And there are too many people. Apart from a silly game we devised with a tennis ball (what else?) on the edge of the Serpentine, we didn't have much fun at all. We pressed on past the Round Pond in flat Kensington Gardens and caught the tube home from Queensway. The station has a lift.

If you live near these parks, then I daresay they'll do for your dog's daily run. But at the weekends why not buy a travelcard and explore London's wild, green places?

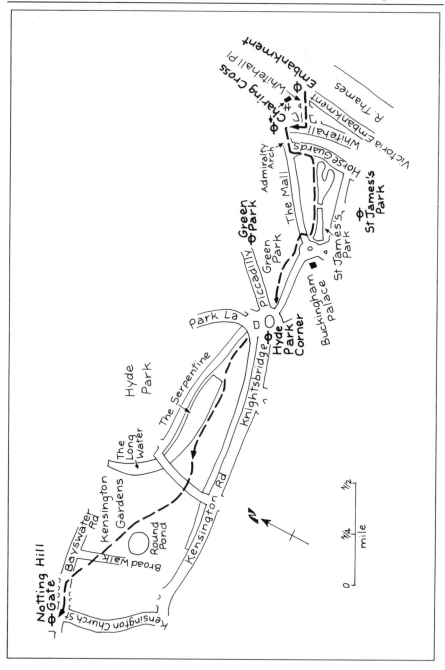

Walk 9: Richmond Circular

This trip beside the Thames and round the Royal Park makes a wonderful day out on a summer weekend. You should allow all day for it. Before you set out make sure you feel comfortable about controlling your dog near horses, deer, sheep and waterfowl. Connects with Walk 13.

Route: Richmond circular walk including Wimbledon Common: with extension Walks to Kew Bridge BR, Twickenham BR, Isleworth BR, Hampton Wick BR and Syon Lane BR.

Distance: 11 miles

Facilities: Loos on the riverside path, in Richmond Park and at Windmill cafe on Wimbledon Common. Cafes and restaurants in Richmond, Richmond Park and Wimbledon Common. Lots of attractive pubs serving meals.

Richmond Park is very large indeed – 2,470 acres (almost 1000 hectares) – so there is plenty of room to be alone with your dog in bracken and woods. Wimbledon Common comes a close second with 1412 acres (565 hectares). Compare that with Hampstead Heath, at 330 hectares, and you will have some idea of the space available for your ramble. So much space that you can be quite a way from other people, roads or houses. So if you're walking solo I recommend a Saturday or Sunday when there should be enough people about to make the walk feel safe without having them impinge on your solitude.

We went to Richmond BR by the North London line. Trains are so much easier than the Tube when you've a dog along. The platforms are less crowded, there's room for him to lie down between the seats and the station approaches involve only a few steps.

At Richmond BR climb the steps and turn left, then right across the zebra over the main road (The Quadrant). Turn right again and take the alley, left, between a branch of Barnard Marcus and a pizzeria called Emandel. In a few metres, turn left along Little Green.

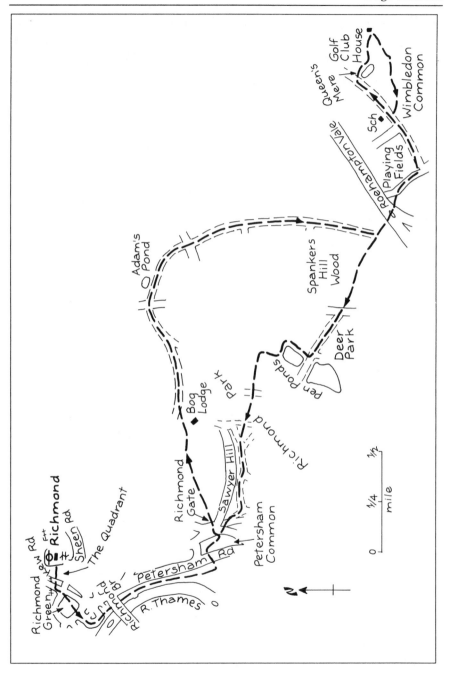

The flat, rather dull, open space of Richmond Green is a few paces ahead to your right; so are lots of signs on lamp posts informing you of the character flaws of dog owners who allow their charges to foul either the pavement or the park – and of the penalties if they do. I can do without this sort of haranguing from the authorities. A simple prohibition is quite sufficient.

You can let your dog off the lead on Richmond Green as long as he is not prone to joining other people's picnics. Stay on the grass – watch out for the traffic on the roads which encircle it – following the curve of the street you have just left (which is also called The Green). When The Green curves right at the far end of the grass, turn left down Friars Lane. At the river bank turn left. Other people, with more reliable dogs, had them running loose; but the banks are steep, there are notices warning you not to swim because of the currents and there are simply too many distractions for a dog who hadn't long been out of Battersea. So Fred stayed on the lead. There are ice cream vans and cafes with tables outside and the Slug and Lettuce pub which appears to be a bikers' haunt. After loos, the river heads right, but you should go straight ahead through a kissing gate into Petersham Fields.

Be warned! These are real fields, grazed by real cows. If the cows aren't there when you visit – absent for milking say – then their pats will be; and you dog will roll in them. Don't fret too much as there are ponds for him to swim in later which will clean him off. But don't release him here if he is even faintly prone to chase other animals. Follow the tarmac path until you are close to the sheep grazing in front of you on the other side of a secure fence and turn left to another kissing gate. Put your dog on the lead to cross Petersham Road (carefully, the bend to the right is blind) and go straight ahead onto a path through Petersham Common. Release your dog. Walk up a steep incline through woods. When the path forks, go right and follow the path to the back of the Star and Garter Home – built in the 1920s to house ex-servicemen with disabilities. Turn right along the narrow gravel path, put your dog on the lead at the edge of the building, turn right up the access road, then left up rustic steps. At the top, turn left into Star and Garter Hill and cross the road at the roundabout to enter Richmond Park via Richmond Gate.

Take the first path sloppy left, with the road (Sawyers Hill) to your right. If you want to explore, don't follow my directions, but wander at will – as long as you remember to head homewards before the gates close (times vary, check the noticeboards at the entrances). There are no restrictions on dogs in the park.

We went through Conduit Wood to a tarmac lane which is the entrance to Bog Lodge. The Metropolitan Police keep their horses here. We headed for the trees to the north, keeping Sawyers Hill just visible to the right. In the woods we ran slap into a large herd of red deer and I hastily put Fred on the lead, decided to press on, then changed my mind as several stags shook their antlers at us. I backtracked, then circled the woods to the north. You would be sensible to do the same – the deer can be dangerous especially in the rutting season. I released Fred and from there we followed the horse ride all the way to East Sheen Gate. When you reach the edge of the car park put your dog on the lead.

And perhaps it is time, as you walk the length of the car park, to hear a little about the history of Richmond Park. The fact that it exists at all is down to the efforts of commoners. In 1750 Amelia, favourite daughter of George II and Ranger of Richmond Park, closed the park to everyone but personal friends. The procedure for obtaining a key to the grounds was so difficult few could achieve it. But John Lewis, a brewer of Richmond, waited until the gates opened to admit a carriage, slipped inside and walked across the park – then claimed a public right of way. We owe the freedom of the park to him.

Walk the length of the car park, keeping it to your left. Cross Sheen Lane, take a few steps left, find the footpath to the right and release your dog. You will soon reach Adam's pond which is shallow at the north end – and therefore ideal for a dip for your dog. Follow the path as it curves south until you see Roehampton Gate to your left. Just before the Gate is a footbridge over Beverley Brook. Don't cross it, stick to the edge of the horse ride, keeping an eye out for horses if your dog is prone to chase them. Cross Sawyers Hill again and continue beside the horse ride. Beverley Brook will run beside you for a while then it veers off to the left. Keep going, ignoring the tempting grassy paths leading up the incline, to reach Robin Hood Gate. By this point you and your dog will already have had a good

Be warned! These are real fields, grazed by real cows.

walk, so you may want to make your leisurely way back to Richmond. If so, follow the directions later in this walk from Robin Hood Gate to Richmond; or explore the wide expanses of the park to the south of our route.

For those of you who continue: put your dog on the lead, cross to the left to the car park. Walk through it to the right and turn left on the road to pass riding stables on your left. You will reach the unpleasant, heavily-trafficked junction of Robin Hood Way and Roehampton Vale. If you dare, cross the footbridge to your right. After my terror of the one over Western Avenue. I prefer to brave the cars. There is a crossing place for horses straight ahead, so I used that. After the road, take the path straight ahead. Release your dog, but be prepared to make way for horses. You are on Wimbledon Common and it feels like real countryside. So it should, the Common has been in existence since at least 675 A.D. Cross a footbridge over Beverley Brook. Turn right, leaving a sports pavilion behind you to your left to follow the horse ride beside the Brook. Beverley Brook is a sleepy sort of stream. It rises in Sutton and – given it is less than fifty feet (15m) above sea level for much of its course – is in no hurry to reach the Thames. Here it is even more leisurely than in Richmond Park, idling its way along a series of meanders. As for the bridle way, it is a serene, green lane surrounded by tall trees. This isn't ancient woodland like the trees of Queen's Wood or Horsenden Wood. Wandsworth – you are now in this borough – has no ancient woodlands at all. Every single scrap of the forest of Middlesex was cleared hundreds of years ago to make room for farming settlements. But 'ancient' woodland means that which dates back to before the 1600s, so some of the trees beneath whose canopy you are now walking are of a pretty good age.

At a v-shaped junction of paths, take the footpath to the left past a 'No horses' sign. It will join a horse ride, called Stag Ride, which you should follow to the left. Pass some allotments to your left – the round yellow face of a giant sunflower leered at us from one of them over a secure fence. Take the next main path right to Queen's Mere and skirt the lake, keeping it to your right. Take the second path left, then right. Stay with the path until you emerge at the open space at the top of the hill and see the white sails of the Windmill ahead. As soon as you emerge onto the grass put your dog on a lead – there are notices asking you to do so. Cross the car park to the cafe. Outside it was a huge horse with a tiny green and brown clad Wimbledon warden perched on top of it like a mounted elf.

The cafe is dog-friendly. There's a big plastic carton of fresh water outside and plenty of tables on the forecourt. Almost everyone at the tables had a dog or two in tow. We met an Irish Wolfhound, two lovely Kerry Blues and a big black chap with a beard whose breed I couldn't pin down. It was all too much for Fred, he retreated under the table and only emerged for the remnant of my buttered scone.

To make the return journey, retrace your steps to Robin Hood Gate and the horse ride on which you were walking before you left Richmond Park. Take the next path to the left – any path will do. Spankers Hill Wood is to your right, more than likely a herd of red deer is to your left. Watch your dog! You are headed up an incline, which is a nice change from the flatness of the northern reaches of the Park, but pretty tiring at this stage of the journey. The scenery and the sky may be adequate compensation. Richmond skies are very wide, far wider than the interrupted ones of the hills north of the Thames. On the day I was there the sky was so wide I had time to figure out under which clump of trees I should shelter – and make it to the trees before the rain fell. Now cut away to the right on a narrow path which leads to the top end of the upper of foul-smelling Pen Ponds. Your dog can have a swim here. After the pond go straight, then right as soon as you find a path to join Queen's Ride. Keep going along the ride to Sawyers Hill, then veer away from it again, south on the horse track. If you look over your shoulder you can see the landmarks of London to the north. Ignore the ride to your left. At the next junction take the ride to your right. It will bring you back to the junction just inside Richmond Gate. From here, retrace your steps to Richmond station. I hope you will come across, as I did, a saxophonist making melancholy music on the river bank as the sun sets over the town.

P.S. If you live in these parts or if you're not tired (not what?) then no need to leave the riverside, you can walk all the way along a footpath to Kew Bridge. I did it once but I don't want to do it again right now.

P.P.S. There's another long walk from Richmond, which I haven't yet done, it goes along the river Crane. Leave Richmond station and cross Kew Road. Go down Park Lane and cross Twickenham Road by the bridge. Turn left and follow the footpath across the Old Deer Park to Richmond Lock. Thereafter you can follow the waymarks (in the shape of a crane, which is a bit like a heron) on a circular walk beside the river or along the Duke of Northumberland's river. BR stations en route are Twickenham and Isleworth.

P.P.P.S. From Richmond there are, of course, lots of other walks. You can go south along the river from Petersham Fields all the way past Ham Riverside Lands to Teddington Lock. Beyond Hampton Wick BR you can walk round Bushy Park (another Royal Park once used for hunting). Or you can stay on the east bank of the river and take the footpath to Kingston Bridge, cross the bridge and follow the tow-path to loop round Hampton Court and northwards past Thames Ditton Island and from thence off the pages of the A to Z. Or you can explore Syon Park to the north of the Old Deer Park. Syon Lane BR station is to the northwest of the park.

Walk 10: Wanstead Park to Leytonstone High Road

*Remarkable for its odd mix of run-down tower blocks and lovely frag-
ments of Epping Forest. It includes a stroll along the Roding river and
some enchanting watery vistas in the grounds of a demolished country
house.*

Route: Wanstead Park BR to Leytonstone High road BR with a diversion
to Manor Park BR and a circular walk around the City of London
Cemetery.

Distance: 6 miles. Circular Walk, 2 miles.

Facilities: No loos. Open air cafe in Wanstead Park (summer only).

Leave Wanstead Park station by a dirty, dilapidated walkway under
the track. Turn right on Woodgrange Road and immediately right
again along Chestnut Avenue. At the next junction bear left and, on
reaching Capel Street, cross it onto the wide open spaces of Wanstead Flats and release your dog. The Flats are the southernmost
portion of Epping Forest, part of the heath of the ancient forest of
Essex. We struck out through the long, yellow grass, skirting football
pitches to the right and keeping well away from the road; there are
major roads running along all the margins of the Flats and I don't
trust Fred to stay off them this early in a walk. The terrain is
featureless apart from improbably placed clumps of trees. We
headed for a batch on the right and went to the left of it, before
picking up a path to the right. The landscape struck me as an odd
obverse of Richmond Park – there people drive through to look at
the scenery, here they drive to get from A to B and ignore the scenery.
Yet, if any one of those motorists stopped and left her car, she'd
discover real countryside under her feet. And real cows.

It wasn't cows I discovered at this point – I discovered Fred rolling
in one of their pats. A new pat, sleek and green and glistening – and

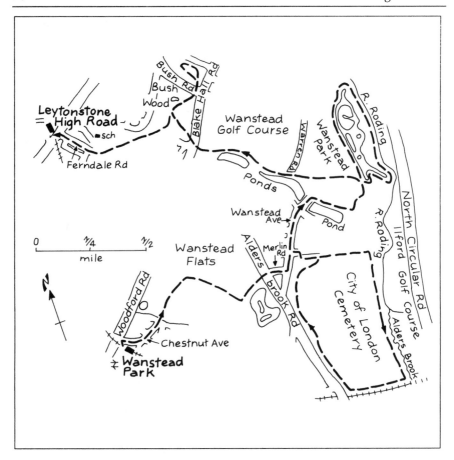

Fred stank. We struck right, across the football pitches, in the direction of the east end of Capel Road – in search of water. On the way we glimpsed in the distance the herd of cows who were responsible for the niff around Fred's neck. We reached Alexandra Lake, which is sunk out of sight in the only discernible hollow on the Flats. It has sloping beaches and two islands, both densely wooded; swans, grebes and coots; and is the biggest lake in Newham. I threw one of Fred's balls into the water so he'd go far enough to get rid of the cow dung. Unfortunately the ball was one he'd punctured with his teeth. It sank – and Fred nearly went down with it, swimming in desperate circles, dipping his nose beneath the surface in search of his treasure. I called him out and we carried on.

I threw one of Fred's balls into the water so he'd go far enough to get rid of the cow dung.

To reach Manor Park BR

Turn right along the shores of Alexandra Lake, pick up the nearest path heading south. Cross Capel Road and go straight ahead down Whitta Road to find, off Forest Drive, the station.

To continue on the main route

Keep Alexandra Lake to your right, cross a car park and put your dog on the lead. Cross Aldersbrook Road and go straight ahead along Merlin Road. Take the next left into Wanstead Park Avenue.

For the circular walk round the City of London Cemetery

Turn right along Empress Avenue. Take the footpath to the right and release your dog. Your route leads you right round the cemetery (which is the second largest in London and has many mature trees plus rhododendrons flowering in late spring) and along a bridle path beside the Alders Brook, which is a branch of the Roding.

To continue on the main route

Ahead of us was a lone, brown cow pottering along the white line in the middle of the road. Wanstead Park Avenue is a street of suburban houses, so she seemed a trifle out of place. She turned right, wandered through some traffic cones, around a bevy of workmen drilling a hole and joined several of her mates headed ... where?

We went straight on. At the top of Wanstead Park Avenue, cross Northumberland Avenue and enter Wanstead Park by a wide lane with Perch Pond to your right and Heronry Pond to your left. Release your dog. At the tip of Perch Pond is a snack bar. Turn right when Perch Pond ends and follow its northern bank. At its eastern end cross a bridleway. To your right, a few metres along is a fenced riding stable manege; a file of horses plodded around it. Go straight across the bridleway and along the footpath into the trees. Turn left along the next bridleway. You are still beneath trees but will shortly reach an open area. I sat down on the long grass there, beneath a shady tree, but leapt up again at the sight of a huge spider perched on my thigh. Panic over, I decided it had been a cricket. Perhaps it was a Roesel's bush cricket which is rare country-wide but has been spotted here.

Go along the clearing, keeping to the right of it, with the white, keeper's lodge to your left, then take a path through trees to the half right. You will shortly reach the wide gravel waterfront of a lovely lake with lots of people fishing. The water has yellow-flowered water lilies and plenty of waterfowl. Turn left beside the water. I put Fred on the lead so as not to disturb the fisherfolk – or the fish.

You will pass Rook Island. At the sign which told me that fishing was no longer permitted I released Fred. Do not do the same if you have a dog who chases ducks or who thinks green slime on water is grass to be walked on. Just past Lincoln Island the water is covered from bank to bank in a seductive carpet of algae looking exactly like a new-mown lawn. Follow the broad track to the north of the lake – you will now have a golf course to your left. The track curves to the right – and brings you to a charming spot on the river Roding where its shallow water runs swiftly past a gently shelving bank. The Roding is an Essex river, more than it is a London one. It rises way out in the countryside, then runs south beside the North Circular and through Barking to the Thames at the Barking Creek Flood Barrier.

As you turn south with the lake to your right, the river winds between high banks. Fred rushed down them several times and returned dripping. When the wide gravel drive bears right, ignore it and stick to the path beside the river. The gravel drive will come close to your path twice, but continue walking along the rough path under branches. Eventually the path will join the gravel drive and lead you to the left round a spur of the lake. Keep following the drive and it will bring you to the bridleway at the bottom of Perch Pond, next to the riding stables. Turn right and walk beside Perch Pond which has a gently sloping beach so your dog can safely enjoy a wallow in the water.

At the upper end of Perch Pond, ignore the footpath by which you arrived and take the wide track which leads ahead, half left. At the next established wide path, turn left. The white, keeper's cottage is to your right. Keep straight ahead along the broad track which soon grazes the northern tip of Heronry Pond and takes you past securely fenced Wanstead Golf Course to your right. Follow the fence as you pass Shoulder of Mutton Pond on your left. Again this pond has a shallow beach – so Fred had a dip. After the pond you plunge into

Reservoir Wood, deep and shady and full of oaks – but not large. As soon as you see traffic ahead put your dog on the lead. Cross Blake Hall Road and turn right. Cross Blake Hall Crescent and just past the bus stop find a winding ride which leads to the left between trees. Release your dog. You are in a small, cut-off corner of Epping Forest. At a fork take a left. Ahead of you is a white post with a black horseshoe painted on it – the symbol in these parts for a bridleway. Stop, turn your head to the left and be surprised – I was – by a white block of flats looming over you. Go straight again and cross two narrow horse rides – the first's called 'The Ride', the second's called 'The Avenue' but there's nothing on the ground to help you make the distinction. Bear left for a few paces along The Avenue and take a winding footpath to the right between the trees.

It is hard to direct you clearly from here; there are no waymarks. But if you follow the wayward path and keep an ear out for traffic, you shouldn't go wrong. Listen for cars running at right angles – that's on Bush Road. Listen for cars running parallel – that's on Blake Hall Road. Aim for the point at which the sounds converge, follow the meandering path and you should emerge from the wood to the left of a one-storey, red brick lodge. Put your dog on the lead and cross Bush Road at the junction with Blake Hall Road – this took us ages, there is no pedestrian crossing. Once over, plunge into the woods straight ahead and follow, to the left, the white posts with the horseshoes. As soon as you can, scramble through the scrub to your right, turn left and follow the white posts to the right, then the left. They will lead you to the major roundabout where Bush Road, Cambridge Park, Hollybush Hill, Whipps Cross Road and Leyton-stone High Road converge. I knew full well that the terrain would improve after this – with lakes and a pond and horse rides which lead to the Forest and the river Ching. But I couldn't face the traffic. I turned for home.

Follow the bridleway along the fence to your left and cut down to the right to the pair of semi-detached woodland cottages just above the junction of Bush Road and Blake Hall Road. Each has a charming, large garden enclosed against the woods. Follow the broad track to the left of the cottages. Put your dog on the lead. Turn right along Blake Hall Road. At the junction cross Bush Road again and go back into the woods alongside the warden's cottage. Follow the path until you reach 'The Avenue'. Turn right.

Keep straight through the trees to emerge into open space with football pitches to your left. White posts with black horseshoes on them indicate the direction you should follow – straight on. It would be hard for anyone to believe this is a bridleway. It is a single-track footpath across football pitches surrounded by a decidedly urban landscape. At the end of it, 'The Avenue' bears right to join Ferndale Road. Pause before you leave 'The Avenue' to look left. First a succession of back gardens with ramshackle fencing separating them from the tract of grassland. Then a terrace of three cottages with ornate doorways faces the open space as though it were a thoroughfare. A few paces further two tower blocks throw long, rectangular shadows over the grass, bringing evening before it is due.

Put your dog on the lead, go straight along Ferndale Road, cross Leytonstone High Road and follow the signs for the station. The trains run every half hour and they're not crowded, even when the rest of London is squashed into the rush hour.

We picknicked on a large, cold gravestone.

Walk 11: Farthing Down circular

A waymarked walk approved by the London Walking Forum. It's only just inside Greater London and joins the North Downs Way. Worth a day out for the hilly wilderness of Happy Valley and the views of London and the Downs. But watch out for sheep and horses and cows – this is the countryside proper.

Route: Farthing Down circular walk from Coulsden South BR.

Distance: 6 miles

Facilities: Loos at the start of the walk. The Fox pub and the Harrow pub are short distances from the route of the walk.

From the station turn south along Downs Road. This walk is amply waymarked and there's a leaflet on it which you can get from Surrey County Council or the London Walking Forum.

But it is worth telling you about because it is charming and the northern half is through wide acres of wonderful fields and woods with no farm animals (but do make sure that both you and your dog stick to the paths across arable land) and only one road to cross to reach Chaldon church which contains the earliest wall painting in England. It's 12th century, depicts the Ladder of Salvation of the Human Soul and is absolutely stunning.

At the entrance to the churchyard we came across a bevy of straw-hatted folk sketching and painting watercolours in thin, old-fashioned tints. We toured the cool interior of the church with Fred on the lead, then picknicked on a large, cold gravestone. There were three of us – we eyed each other's sandwiches while Fred chewed a tennis ball at our feet.

The southern half of the walk is less good for dogs. It does offer a panoramic view across the Surrey Hill Area of Outstanding Natural Beauty (and an opportunity to join the North Downs way and walk your way into the real countryside), but on the return journey there are horses and sheep behind fences which would not deter any dog;

and there is a stretch of lane walking before you return to woods. The full walk is 7 miles long.

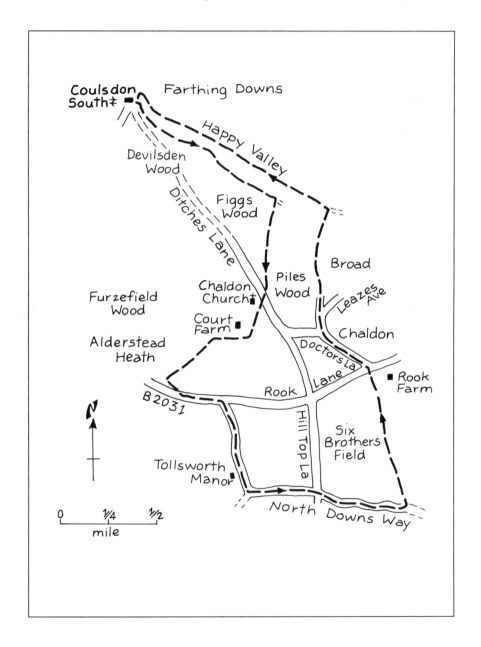

Walk 12: Morden

Along the banks of the Wandle – an intriguing mix of linear parks, industrial estates and old mills. Connects with Walk 13.

Route: Morden to Colliers Wood, Haydons Road BR or Earlsfield BR or Wandsworth Town BR and circular walk from Morden Passing Mitcham Junction BR and Mitcham BR. with extension walks to Beddington Lane BR, Hackbridge BR, Carshalton BR and Carshalton Beeches BR.

Distance: 3 miles. Circular Walk, 5½ miles.

Facilities: Loos in Morden Hall Park and Oaks Park. Cafes in Morden Hall Park and Oaks Park. The Riverside Free House. The Royal Six Bells pub. Open air shellfish stand outside the Goat pub.

At the top of the short flight of stairs, turn left from Morden tube on London Road, left at the roundabout along Morden Road and cross at the lights. A few steps further, enter Morden Hall Park to the right and release your dog. Follow the path straight ahead beside the river. On the other bank you can see, through the trees, the Hall, which was built in 1770. In 1941 its owner, Gilliat Hatfeild, left 125 acres (50 hectares) of the estate to the National Trust.

You must pick up after your dog in this lovely park. The National Trust support responsible dog ownership but are finding the number of dogs who visit Morden Hall a problem. As Paul Rutter, the head warden of the property, pointed out: many parks have closed their doors to dogs because owners won't stick to the very reasonable rules. Please don't be the reason Morden Hall Park introduces a ban.

To your left is marshland which the Wandle used to flood before the National Rivers Authority instigated electronic control of the water level. If you turn left across the marshlands you can cross the footbridge to Bunce's Meadow and follow the path to Deen City Farm (where your dog must be on a lead).

To follow the Wandle trail north, cross the river by the footbridge

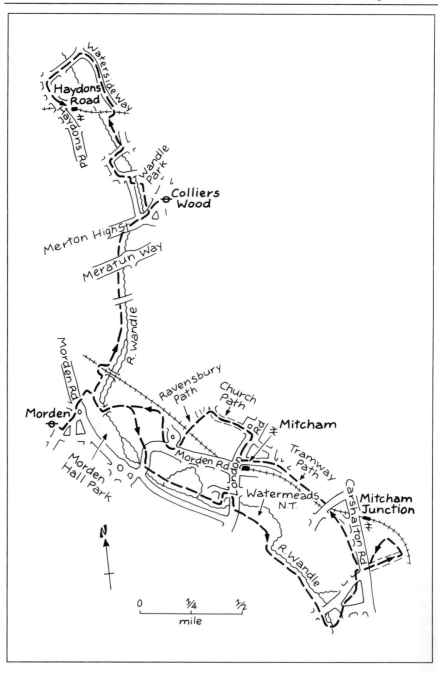

to the right. There used to be watercress beds here and lavender. Turn left over another footbridge.

The Wandle runs for about ten miles from its source in Beddington Park to the Thames. It was the cradle of the Industrial Revolution. It powered woollen mills and snuff mills and all sorts of other mills – there used to be nearly seventy of them along its banks. Some of them still exist. The Wandle is also the reason why Wandsworth is so called. I was told these facts by Richard Kew, the knowledgeable expert on London's rivers at the National Rivers Authority. He had another message. He wanted me to look out, on my excursions, for pollution in the capital's waterways. For you to look out for it too. You can phone him and tell him of any nasties on a 24-hour Freephone, 0800 807060.

Meanwhile, at a gate in a wooden fence you may want to put your dog on the lead – the path beyond the fence runs beside the railway which is protected only by a low iron railing topped with sharp spikes. Go through the gate, turn right and cross the line by an elderly footbridge. Release your dog and cross a bridge over the water beside a waymark in the shape of a water-wheel. The path runs through scrub, curving past a securely fenced riding stable. At a green signpost pointing left to Merton Abbey Mills put your dog on the lead and walk along the road, passing a car park and a pylon (pylons are quite a feature of this walk). Cross Windsor Avenue (the road is throated to slow cars), release your dog and continue on the path. Here the river is no longer slow and gentle but wide and fast flowing. There's a frothy waterfall, then, on the opposite bank, the Riverside Free House with a big garden, followed by a market. You can reach both by a footpath just before Merantun Way.

Put your dog on the lead, cross the busy road by the pedestrian crossing, go under a brick arch, then across Station Road. The path continues a couple of steps to the right. I kept Fred on the lead for the first stretch because the river is a wide, swift channel at the bottom of a deep cutting and the fence beside it is low. But soon the banks are shallow again with a patch of grass beside them – so I let him free. At the Sainsbury Savacentre put your dog on the lead, follow the path as it curves right and join Merton High Street. Ignore the Wandle Trail signpost and cross the road by the pedestrian crossing in front of you. Turn right, cross the river, pass the Royal

Six Bells pub, turn left into Wandle Park and release your dog. This is a poop scoop park.

To reach Colliers Wood

Don't enter the park, continue a few paces along the road and the station is in front of you. It has fixed stairs between the escalators.

To continue on the Wandle Trail

Follow the tarmac path across Wandle Park. The park is small and flat and remarkable only for its huge, odd, white statues. The first is a memorial to the generous chap from Birmingham who gave the park to local people. The second, to the right of the path, is a giant jug, about five feet high, with two highly-coloured fish moulded on its handle. Shortly after the jug, take a left fork in the path towards the river – which you can hear rushing along behind a screen of greenery. The bridge across it is hidden until the last minute and there's a road on the other side, so keep an eye on your dog. At the bridge, snap on his lead and cross the river. Turn right along the pavement of Wandle Bank (a road).

Follow the Walk signpost left along South Road, then right into East Road, right into deserted North Road. Cross the river, follow another signpost into Wandle Park Nature Reserve and release your dog. The river runs to its left, but do not follow it; if you do you will reach a dead end. Instead take the central path – on which we encountered the most aggressive dog we have ever met in all our walks – a German Shepherd so set on eating Fred alive that its owner (a tough-looking heavy of the kind usually accompanied by a muzzled Pitbull) had his work cut out hanging onto its choke chain. We hurried on. It was four o'clock and the autumn sun was slipping towards the rooftops to the left.

Just before an information board, turn right along the path and walk through a wooden gate to a wide cycleway. Turn left under the railway bridge. To your right are factories, to your left rough undergrowth. Also to your right are cartoon signs on lamp posts which warn that the penalty for dog fouling is £500! You've a way to walk along this quiet path. When you hear the traffic of Plough Lane ahead, put your dog on the lead.

. . . the most aggressive dog we have ever met

To reach Haydons Road BR

Turn left on Plough Lane, left down Havelock Road, right into Kohat Road, left into Haydons Road.

That's how we went home, but you needn't if you're not tired. The Secretary of the Wandle Group, a voluntary organisation which keeps an eye on the river, told me that you can follow the Trail from Plough Lane – the entrance to the path is to the left of the river – to the north end of Weir Road. From there it's a short walk across the river, left along Summerley Street with your dog on the lead and left again into Garratt Lane to find Earlsfield BR. Or keep going along Garratt Lane to a street called Bendon Valley on your left. Turn into it, bear right at the bottom and cross the footbridge to your left over the river. You will be in King George's Park. This is a Wandsworth park. Wandsworth has the most comprehensive policy on dogs of any of the boroughs I contacted. It supplies the most information too. Particularly useful is its map of poop scoop parks. This shows where there are no restrictions on dogs, where you are obliged to clean up and the areas (usually formal gardens and children's play areas) where no dogs are allowed. Oh and in Wandsworth there are no penalties if your dog uses the gutter. King George's Park has a large poop scoop area at its southern end. Cross Kimber Road and you are still in such an area. A little further north is an unrestricted area, then a poop scoop stretch threading its way between areas in which dogs are banned.

To the north of King George's Park you can walk, with your dog on the lead, along Buckhold Road, turn right into Wandsworth High Street, left into Wandsworth Plain alongside the Youngs Brewery, right into Armoury Way, and left alongside the river again. From the end of The Causeway which runs beside the Wandle you can see across the Thames, but have no access to it. You can follow The Causeway to the east, turn right down Smugglers Way, cross Swandon Way and find Wandsworth Town BR.

Instead of doing this and on another day we went south from Morden along the Wandle on a circular walk.

Morden circular walk

Parts of this walk can be very isolated, so it's not ideal for a solo excursion.

Enter Morden Hall Park as before, press ahead and cross the bridge to the right. Ignore the bridge to the left and cross the stream. Fred had a dip here from the low bank to the right of the bridge.

You are in a picnic area so dogs must be on leads. The path leads away from the Hall towards a charming white-painted iron bridge over the river. Cross the bridge. Should you want to know more about the history and ecology of the estate, don't cross the bridge but turn right with your dog on the lead. You will pass the stable block. It has a weather vane in the shape of the brown trout which used to throng the Wandle's waters. To your left is a water wheel and snuff mill which is now an Environmental centre. The original water wheel is still there. It was used for grinding tobacco into snuff until 1922.

But we pressed on over the white bridge and into the meadows, where you can release your dog. Do the same and you will walk along an avenue of lime and horse chestnut trees. Ignore the buildings on the skyline and the distant roar of traffic and you could easily be in a country estate. The meadowland has been cared for using traditional methods for over a century. The grass has never been ploughed or sprayed with artificial fertilisers, but was grazed by deer and then dairy cattle until the 1970s. The National Trust plans to re-introduce grazing to maintain the meadows in the traditional way – when this happens they will require dogs to be kept on leads near the animals.

Continue along the main path. Fred met lots of other dogs here. I was disappointed to find all their owners had a down on them playing and called their animals sharply, snapped on their leads and dragged the poor mutts away. Fred was five months out of Battersea before he learnt to play with other dogs. Now it's one of the delights of my walks to watch him and a new mate boxing and feinting and taking turns to chase and be chased in great, loopy circles.

At the high wooden door at the end of the path put your dog on the lead and step out onto Morden Road. Cross the road and turn right. Take the tarmac path to the left of the river and release your dog. Soon, to your left, is the green space of Ravensbury Park. Continue alongside the river past a bridge to the right and a Wandle Trail information board. The river is deeper than it was in Morden Hall Park and there are plenty of waterfowl, so watch your dog. When the path leads over a bridge to the right, follow it. To your left is an area of dangerous deep water with a sign stuck in it telling you that that's what it is.

Cross another bridge and emerge in the gardens of a housing estate. The path turns left between trees with a high brick wall to your right and it is time to put your dog on the lead. Cross Bishopford Road and turn right. Ignore the Wandle Trail sign which points to Willow Lane, cross the river by the brick bridge and take the waymarked path beyond Watermeads Nature Reserve. The path is fenced on both sides so you can release your dog. Watermeads is owned by the National Trust and only accessible by appointment (and I very much doubt that dogs would be welcome). Peer through the trees to see a row of white-painted, clapboarded houses. There are playing fields to the right and soon the fence is replaced by a ditch.

Your path leads into woodland. When you emerge from it Poulter Park is to your right. After the curve in the river go through a kissing gate, cross a small, brick bridge and put your dog on the lead as the path becomes a lane (Watermead). Turn left on Goat Lane. If you can trust your dog on a (fairly large) open space which is unfenced and surrounded by roads, then cross Goat Lane onto Mill Green. There are paths crisscrossing this flat grassland and bridges over the river. Press ahead parallel to Goat Lane.

Pass the Goat pub on your left, cross Carshalton Road, take the path directly ahead across Mitcham Common and release your dog. The path runs through scrub and woodland and when we were there it was deserted. Continue on it to a T junction of paths with a railway bridge to your right and a golf course ahead.

To reach Beddington Lane BR

Turn right and the path will take you to the station.

To continue on the main route

Turn left, Take the next rough path left and follow the line of trees back to Carshalton Road. Your dog will have plenty of opportunity on the way to enjoy the yellow undergrowth. Shortly before Carshalton Road put him on the lead.

To reach Mitcham Junction BR

Turn right and continue until you reach the station.

To continue on the main route

Cross the road and find, almost directly ahead and behind a bus stop, a concrete path signposted, 'Public Footpath to Mitcham'. Take it and release your dog. The path runs between high fences. A little later some of the gardens to the right have no fences. After building works to your left, put your dog on the lead, climb the steps to Willow Lane and turn right over a humpbacked bridge. Turn left, cross the road, descend the steps onto the footpath and release your dog. The securely fenced railway is on your left. Cross the end of the cul-de-sac of Caesar's Way – I didn't bother putting Fred on the lead here – and continue along the path. It's called Tramway Path. Soon it runs beside The Close with only a gappy hedge to prevent your dog dashing into the road. So I put Fred on the lead. The Close, once you cross Bramcote Avenue, becomes Mitcham Park (which is a street, not a park).

To reach Mitcham BR

Turn left along London Road and find, in a few paces, the station.

To continue on the main route

At London Road turn right. It's bordered by horrid-looking blocks of red-brick flats. Cross the road as soon as you are able – it's busy. Turn right again. A few metres on to the left go down Church Path which is actually a narrow street. Don't release your dog until the street (in a metre or so) becomes a path. It runs alongside a playing field. When Church Path the path hits Church Path the street, put your dog on the lead and turn right, ignoring the footpath to the left. A few steps further, cross to your left and go down the footpath opposite. Keep your dog on the lead. Cross deserted Benedict Road and continue along the footpath. You can release him here if you want, but I felt I needed Fred's protection at my fingertips. You are walking between industrial sites and we saw no other people. Cross the railway bridge and put your dog on the lead. Turn right on Morden Road, cross Deer Park Gardens and a few paces later, just before the Surrey Arms, turn right along a footpath and release your dog. The path leads back into the meadows of Morden Hall Park.

P.S. Just as you can walk north of Haydons Road BR so can you walk south along the Wandle all the way to its source in Beddington Park, then catch the train home from Hackbridge BR. Or you can walk to Carshalton Park where there is a heritage centre with information about the river – and catch the train from Carshalton BR or Carshalton Beeches.

Your route will take you to Wilderness Island which is by all accounts a lovely spot. You can also go south from Carshalton Beeches, down Beeches Lane which becomes Woodmansterne Lane and, after a mile, join the Sutton Countryside Walk which begins at Oaks Park. This is a waymarked route (part of which crosses fields which are grazed by horses) of about five miles with a cafe and toilets en route. Happy walking!

Walk 13: Gunnersbury to East Putney

From the classic formality of the grounds of Palladian Chiswick House to a long stretch of deserted riverside and finally to the heathlands at Barnes and Putney. There is a stretch of road walking at the outset, but it is well worth it to reach the delightful contrasts in the terrain to come. Connects with Walks 9 and 12.

Route: Gunnersbury or Chiswick Park BR or Turnham Green to East Putney, passing Chiswick BR, Barnes Bridge BR and Barnes BR. Diversions available to Hammersmith, Ravenscourt Park, Goldhawk Road, Putney Bridge, Putney BR and Richmond.

Distance: 8½ miles

Facilities: Loos in the grounds of Chiswick House, in Furnivall Gardens, Ravenscourt Park, Barnes Common and Putney Heath. Cafes at Chiswick House, Ravenscourt Park. Pubs with gardens along the route. Open air snack bars at Putney Heath and East Putney station.

We started from Gunnersbury station but you could just as easily set out from Chiswick Park BR and thread your way through the streets south of Chiswick High Road to join us; or from Turnham Green cross Chiswick Common and head down Fisher's Lane, then Duke Road and enter the grounds of Chiswick House from the north eastern end. Turnham Green has stairs.

At Gunnersbury station go along the walkway through the station building and turn right on the short, securely fenced footpath. Cross Gunnersbury Road by the zebra and go straight ahead along Harvard Road. Take the subway to the right under the Great West Road, turn next left, next right and right again into Fauconberg Road. Cross Sutton Court to continue straight along Staveley Road. After you cross Park Road, cross Staveley Road to the left to find the imposing gates which are the entrance to the grounds of Chiswick House.

Release your dog in the woodland. It's called The Wilderness and you must clean up after him in it. Take the left fork of the path beside

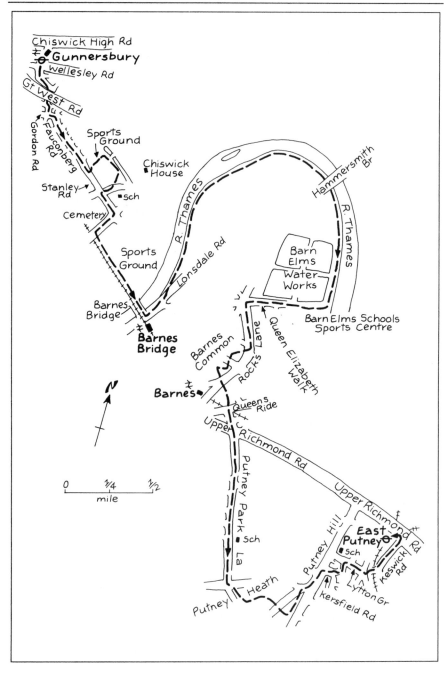

loos and through the trees to the narrow lake which bisects the grounds. It isn't really a lake. Originally it was the Bollo Brook, a tidal creek of the Thames. When Lord Burlington had the gardens laid out he incorporated the creek into his design. The more formal gardens and the house itself are on the opposite bank. The gardens were created by William Kent for Lord Burlington between about 1718 and the 1740s and were the first ambitious design in the new style of the Picturesque. This was the interim stage between the very formal gardens of the Tudors and Stuarts and the informal country-side effects of Capability Brown and his followers.

On this side the deep water is fenced by a low railing. Turn right alongside it. You will shortly see on the opposite bank the Ionic Temple (which was designed by Inigo Jones and is an amphitheatre surrounding a circular pool in which stands an obelisk), the gardens and the ornamental stonework in them. Even on this wilder side of the water there are contrived views a-plenty: clearings with vistas, tracks devised to draw the eye to a building or an obelisk. Take the second tarmac path right to a tall column. Stop and look back. You are standing on a point at which three paths meet. This design is called a *patte d'oie* (goose foot), because of its shape and was designed to lead the eye to one or another feature of the garden. The central path leads to the Temple. Put your dog on the lead and exit the grounds to the left. Turn right along Burlington Lane and left at Staveley Road to walk between allotments and school playing fields. The allotments give way to Chiswick Cemetery from which dogs are banned. Turn right at the end of the cemetery and walk its length along Great Chertsey Road. Immediately before the railway bridge turn right, descend the steps and release your dog on the securely fenced path.

To reach Chiswick BR

Turn right along the path. At Russell Kerr Close turn right, left on Burlington Lane, cross the footbridge and you are in Station Approach.

To continue on the main route

Turn left under the grey concrete railway bridge and go straight, ignoring the narrow paths to the left until you see a road directly ahead. Put your dog on the lead, cross a cobbled lane and walk straight along the road. When the road bends left, go straight on the well-fenced path to the Thames. If your dog is sensible you can release him here, to turn right and go over Barnes Bridge by the footway. I kept Fred on the lead – although the bridge is fenced, the fence isn't high enough for my peace of mind. Ahead the riverside 'town' of Barnes looks like a dignified seaside resort with Regency villas facing the promenade along the waterfront. Descend the bridge still on the footway.

To reach Barnes Bridge BR

The charming station is straight ahead.

To continue on the main route

Turn left, go down the steps, cross The Terrace and turn right along the path by the river. You can't release your dog here: the path is merely a raised pavement with nothing more than a handrail between you and the traffic. Barnes is every bit as delightful as it looked from the bridge, with crooked alleys snaking south between the waterfront houses and flowers in tubs and hanging baskets. Once upon a time Barnes was a summer resort for well-off Londoners – I can quite see why.

For a short cut to Barnes BR

Turn right along the High Street and left on Church Road. Pass St Mary's church which has a fifteenth century tower, continue past shops to a group of houses round a chestnut tree and the Sun Inn. Cross the road to Barnes Pond, then the footbridge to Barnes Common. Take any footpath to the right to find Station Road and turn right along it to the station.

To continue on the main route

At the junction with Barnes High Street, continue straight beside the Thames, passing the Waterman's Arms, the Bull's Head and a police station. Opposite Gerard Road to the right, your path leaves the main road and heads across grass to the left. Don't release your dog yet, the traffic is still close. At the gate to Leg O'Mutton Nature Reserve you can dispense with the lead – but don't go into the nature reserve! Instead stay on the track beside the river. It's a deserted walk through woodland with grey, muddy banks shelving gently down to the water. The authorities – along with the Ramblers Association and the London Walking Forum – have recently opened a path running right through the capital on both sides of the river. It covers 175 miles from the Thames Barrier to the Thames Head. But not all of it is ideal for walking with your dog.

I know this for a fact. One winter afternoon Fred and I returned to London Bridge after an outing in Camberwell to find the tube station thronged with men in suits running for their connections – and no stairs, only escalators. I couldn't face descending into what must surely be a dog's equivalent of Hell. Instead we walked across the bridge to the north bank and along the river path west to Blackfriars – but found none of the route pleasant. I'm sure it's a delight for the city folk clustered around waterfront wine bars, but in between there were dark, deserted stretches and the whole is concrete-surfaced. It's simply not suitable for dogs, except perhaps the smallest of toys.

Which is utterly unlike the track on which we are walking today. Fred took a dip in the Thames – his first ever. You will reach Chiswick Eyot (Eyot is Old English for small island). There are several stands of reeds on the side of the island facing your path, but most of the Eyot is covered with willow pollards. Until this century the island was used for cultivating osiers: willows were planted and cut each year to produce the osiers out of which baskets were woven. The baskets were used to carry fruit and vegetables from local market gardens to the city centre.

Pass an adventure playground to your right and a track leading alongside it. Hammersmith Bridge is ahead.

To reach Hammersmith

At the bridge take the track to the right and, with your dog on the lead, climb up to the bridge. Cross it by the footway to its left and continue straight under the flyover until you reach the station. There are walk-ways, lifts or stairs to all the platforms.

To reach Ravensourt Park

Just before the end of Hammersmith Bridge on the northern bank, descend the steps to your left which are bounded by a black, iron railing. At the bottom, turn left again, then right alongside the river. There are two pleasant pubs here, both of which serve meals which you can eat at tables outside on the flagstones. Beyond the pubs, but still on the waterfront is the green space of Furnivall Gardens. The Gardens aren't large (1.6 hectares) but they are screened from the noise of the traffic on the Great West Road by a hedge and the view of the river is pleasant. Unfortunately you are unlikely to find a bench on which to sit as almost every one is occupied, night or day, by a sleeping homeless person. You are now in the London Borough of Hammersmith & Fulham in which all dog faeces wherever they fall (including the gutter) must be collected and stowed in bins. And you are not permitted to let your dog off the lead – a stupid rule, the reasoning behind which I cannot fathom.

At the end of the Gardens, turn right along a tarmac path, then left along the alley which leads past the Dove pub (no seats outside, I'm afraid). Follow the concrete path beside the river to turn right at Rivercourt Road, right again on the Great West Road and left through the subway. Emerge to go straight ahead along King Street. Cross the road to a crowd of people spilling from the pavement. What are they doing? They are inspecting the cards in the window of a corner store which must come a close second to the classified section of *The Standard* for finding a bedsit or a flatshare. Go past the crowd along Ravenscourt Road. The tube station, which has stairs, is to your right.

To reach Goldhawk Road

Go under the bridge and turn left along the footpath to enter Ravenscourt Park. It's one of the largest parks in the borough but it's not much fun for your dog. Dogs must be kept on leads. Iron railings divide the potentially pleasant place into ghettos. In some only people are allowed, some are designed for young children, some for slightly older ones. And there is of course, at the northwest end of the park, a fenced area for dogs. In it you must pick up after your dog. I'm all in favour of that – but why segregate dogs from people?

A dog which isn't regularly subjected to the hazards of everyday life – noisy ball games, whizzing roller blades, the exploratory finger of a toddler on his nose – can become an instant menace when confronted by them for the first time. Dogs thrive from learning to obey their owners in the real world. Other boroughs – Lambeth for instance – have recognised that special dog exercise areas encourage fighting between the dogs – from boredom I should think.

There is a cafe in Ravenscourt Park, but you're not allowed to take your dog into the fenced area around it even if he's on the lead. A pity, because the cafe serves good food (especially the soups), has a pleasant, relaxed atmosphere and all the day's papers laid out on a table.

Exit the park beyond the cafe just to the south of the scented garden, turn left on Paddenswick Road, cross by the zebra, and turn left again to reach Goldhawk Road at the roundabout. Turn right on Goldhawk Road. The station has stairs.

To continue on the main route

Follow the riverside track past the Barn Elms reservoirs. Pass a memorial to Steve Fairbairn, famous oarsman and coach-founder of the Head of the River race. The memorial is exactly one mile from the start of the University Boat Race. At Queen Elizabeth Walk turn right through the gate. You can keep going along the riverside path, from thence along the Embankment and cross Putney Bridge to find Putney Bridge tube (which has lifts and stairs) or turn right down East Putney High Street to find Putney BR. But we're going to East Putney – by the scenic route.

To your right are high fences protecting the reservoirs, to your left an even higher fence round playing fields. A flock of Canada geese roams the fields – I presume to keep the grass down. After tennis courts (Fred's ears perked up) Queen Elizabeth Walk becomes a lane, so put your dog on the lead to pass Barn Elms Scouts Group HQ. At the end of the lane is the Red Lion pub with a garden. At busy Rocks Lane turn left and walk the length of fenced, private playing fields. Just after the pavilion you can see Beverley Brook which we last came across on Walk 9 flowing through Wimbledon Common. At the junction of Ranelagh Road (where there are loos) cross Rocks

Lane and take the tarmac path straight ahead onto Barnes Common. Release your dog, but keep an eye on him as the common is very small. It's pleasant though and its yellow and green heathland is a delightful contrast to the watery vistas of the Thames-side path.

Take the first tarmac path to the left. When you are within sniffing distance of Mill Hill Road put your dog on the lead, cross and release him again taking the footpath straight ahead. At the end of a group of houses to your right and after the slip road which circles them, turn right along any rough path and, at the corner of the houses, left along a tarmac path. At Rocks Lane put your dog on the lead to cross, then release him and take the path straight ahead. If you want to take in Putney Common keep going to cross Commons Road and explore the 43 acres (17 hectares) of grassland beyond it. To follow us, watch for a football ground to the right, cross it and take the rough track at the bottom to the junction of Commons Road and Queen's Ride. Watch your dog near the traffic or put him on the lead. Turn abrupt right, release him and go along the enclosed path (the fences are swathed in ivy) parallel to Queen's Ride.

To reach Barnes BR

Turn right before the bridge and carry on along the path to the station.

To continue on the main route

Put your dog on the lead at the steps to the left, climb them, turn right and cross the railway. Cross Queen's Ride to the left and go down Gypsy Hill to cross Upper Richmond Road (the South Circular) and follow a sign pointing to St. Margaret's Church and a second sign on a gate warning you that the road ahead is private. It is also a greenway managed by Wandsworth, which borough you have now entered. Remember their policy on dog mess! The greenway is a poop scoop area. It is also another complete change of terrain, rather like a lane through a quiet village. The Pleasaunce, an open space like a village green, is soon to your right. There's the occasional exit to the housing estate on the right, but otherwise the walk is securely fenced all the way to Putney Heath Road. When you see a lodge ahead put your dog on the lead, cross Putney Heath Road and, keeping Telegraph Road to your right, enter Putney Heath and release your dog.

To reach Richmond

It'll be miles before you get there, but you might want to try if you've only just started out, if you're very ambitious or if you own a Dalmatian. Take the track to the right of Telegraph Road and follow the horse ride left to join Roehampton Lane as soon as you can. Once across, thread your way through the suburban streets ahead to enter Richmond Park and follow the directions in Walk 9 to reach distant Richmond.

To continue on the main route

Take the right fork on a narrow, rudimentary path which runs roughly parallel to Telegraph Road. This is a woodland track marred only by the closeness of the traffic. At the end of a fenced garden with a neatly-clipped hedge, turn left through the woods. Take the next right fork. Ignore all tracks to right and left and when you see the road ahead put your dog on the lead to cross Wildcroft Road. Release him and go straight into a rough, grassy space. To your right is a belt of trees into which Fred rushed, then returned to find me inspecting a wooden bench. It was probably dedicated to Sydney A Tucker or Sydney A Lucker, but defacers have been at work and amended his name to something unprintable. Cross the grass – there is no track, just follow your ears towards the next road. When you reach the end of the trees, a bridleway leads to the right. This hugs Tibbets Ride and if you followed it you would shortly reach the major junction of Tibbets Corner and from there find the south section of Putney Heath, progress to Wimbledon Common and join Walk 9.

But for this walk, go left parallel with the main road (Tibbet's Ride). Put your dog on the lead as soon as the road seems close enough for this to be imperative. Keep straight to reach a bus terminus and an open air stall which sells burgers as well as hot drinks and ice cream. There is a newspaper stall next to it. The Green Man pub directly across the road has a garden into which dogs on leads are allowed. Turn right along Putney Heath Road and cross

Putney Hill by the pedestrian crossing. Turn left, take the next right – Kersfield Road – and the next left. The quiet street soon curves left into a housing estate garden, then left between stretches of grass which your dog must not foul. You will join Lytton Grove via Redgate Terrace. Turn right and walk to the bend in the road opposite Holmbush Road. Cross Lytton Grove, take the footpath to the left of the premises of the 1st Cadet Detachment and, keeping your dog on the lead, cross the railway. Turn left on Keswick Road, left on Upper Richmond Road and go under the bridge to East Putney tube. To reach Putney BR continue along Upper Richmond Road.

Postscript: If you are travelling home, as we were, by the Northern line, then there's no interchange that I can find at Embankment which doesn't involve an escalator. After several forays through tunnels I resolved to carry Fred. For the first minute or so he kept still, delighted at the unexpected cuddle, then realised he couldn't escape – and struggled. The early afternoon commuters certainly enjoyed the spectacle of the pair of us – but I won't be going that way again.

Commuters certainly enjoyed the spectacle of the pair of us.

Walk 14: Arnos Grove to High Barnet

A walk along Pymmes Brook. It crosses wide meadows with views of rolling countryside in the vast acres of Trent Park; and the rough heathland of Monken Hadley Common. But this isn't real countryside so there are none of its drawbacks. If your dog doesn't like road walking and you have a car, then best to drive straight to Oakwood or Cockfosters and take up the Walk from there. You — and he — will be rewarded with miles of freedom and the kind of terrain of which every dog, when he twitches in his sleep, is undoubtedly dreaming. Connects with Walks 1 and 7.

Route: Arnos Grove to High Barnet with diversions to Southgate, Oakleigh Park BR, Oakwood, Cockfosters and New Barnet BR.

Distance: 8 miles. Extension to West Finchley, 3½ miles.

Facilities: Loos in Arnos Park and Trent Park. Cafe and ice cream van (summer) in Trent Park. Pubs along the route.

Arnos Grove is above ground and has fixed stairs. Turn right and right again along Brookdale to find the entrance to Arnos Park to the right. Release your dog (you must pick up after him) and go straight ahead on the path under the viaduct over which the Piccadilly line runs. On the other side are loos. Cross the green iron bridge over Pymmes Brook and turn left along the path beside the viaduct. At a Pymmes Brook waymark put your dog on the lead and cross Waterfall Road. Enter the green space ahead – also decorated with a waymark – and release your dog. You are in a thin green walkway with a high fence between you and the traffic of Hampden Way. After the Great Northern Cemetery follow the path to the right away from the Brook between trees. At the top of the gentle slope follow the Pymmes Brook waymark to Ossidge Lane and put your dog on the lead to cross the road. A narrow strip of green on either side of the Brook leads between East Walk and West Walk. There are no paths on the grass and no fences. Either walk on the pavement or through the wet grass so your dog can run free – but do watch for traffic if he is inclined to dash off. At the end of the strip of grass,

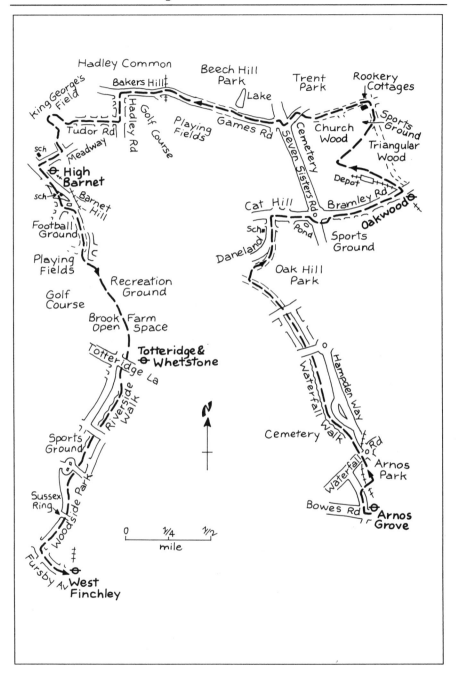

put your dog on the lead to cross Parkside and go along the driveway ahead which is the entrance to Oakhill Park. Once you have passed the car park you can release your dog and go straight along the path. Oakhill Park is formal and you must clean up after your dog; but there is plenty of space for him to run.

To reach Oakleigh Park BR

At the bridge ignore the paths sharp right and left and the one which leads directly forward. Instead take the path sloppy left to reach Church Hill Road. Put your dog on the lead, cross the road and go down the road opposite. Turn right on Cedar Avenue, continue along it as it becomes Rosslyn Avenue, turn left down Oakhurst Avenue and go straight across the walkway to the station.

To continue on the main route

When you see a football pitch on your right leave the tarmac path and strike across the grass to the right, uphill to find a track leading past the backs of houses. Some of the gardens aren't securely fenced, so watch your dog doesn't trespass. After a steep, wooded gully to your right, take the right fork in the track with a board fence to your left and emerge in a green, open space. Put your dog on the lead as you approach the road in front of you (Daneland), turn right and, at the top, right again along major Cat Hill. You've a fair way to walk before, at the roundabout, you pass a pond inhabited by umpteen mallards. Cross Chase Side straight ahead, take a few steps to the right and join the track which runs to the left of playing fields. Best to keep your dog on the lead here, you aren't far from the traffic. The track joins Bramley Road just before a white house with black shutters. Continue along the road (again, it's a fair way) to cross Chase Road by the pedestrian crossing, turn sharp left and cross Bramley Road to reach the entrance to Trent Country Park.

To reach Oakwood tube

Don't cross Bramley Road and the station is right in front of you. It has a a flower stall outside and a short flight of steps to the trains

To continue on the main route

Release your dog and take the path straight ahead. Trent Country

Park is one of the few surviving remnants of the Royal Hunting Forest of Enfield Chase. It covers 470 acres (188 hectares) of woods and meadows. Near the house at its centre is an ornamental water garden, but the rest of the 'park' is utterly lacking in formality. Trent Park is in Enfield, a borough which welcomes dogs in all its country parks and open spaces. The only restrictions are that they must be on leads near farm animals and should not swim in lakes for fear of disturbing wildfowl or endangering the dogs (nice of them to think of the dogs). There is no requirement to pick up after your dog in this huge expanse of countryside.

The Park is worthy of an entire day out. At its north eastern end there's a two and a quarter mile bridleway running through dense Moat Wood and Williams Wood. You can walk through them with your dog as long as he is safe near horses. The woods are large and deep and mysterious and I walked them with Fred on a wet spring weekday when we were fed up with entire world – and with each other.

But we're not going to the woods on this winter afternoon. Instead follow the path to a pine wood, watching out for traffic on the lane to your right. Cross a stream by a footbridge. The silver trains of the Piccadilly line run to your left. Follow the path, which is now fenced on both sides, past private farmland and sharp right into an open meadow. Continue straight along the path – there are waymarks to indicate that this is a cycleway – and cross another stream by a footbridge.

To reach Cockfosters

Follow the waymarks straight ahead and hug the railway line through three meadows until your path turns right, away from it. Carry on through dense vegetation. Fred even forgot about his tennis balls, he was so busy scenting rabbits. Pass Islington Cemetery to your right and a car park to your left, put your dog on the lead and the station is to your left. It has stairs.

To continue on the main route

Turn sharp right down the hill keeping the hedgerow to your right. At the bottom, cross the bridge over another stream and a second bridge into the field to the right. Triangular Wood is to your right. Head straight across the field (there's no track). At the top pass a gate onto a lane to the right (Snakes Lane). Go straight ahead along the path. Be careful your dog isn't too near the lane, it's unfenced. Put your dog on the lead to cross a small car park and turn left on Snakes Lane keeping an eye out for traffic. Pass the sports ground to the left and take the private road immediately to your left. Once past Rookery Cottages release your dog at the wooden gate and walk along an avenue between deep woods – I bet your dog will enjoy them. Keep straight, ignoring all turnings, to reach a tapping rail for blind people to the left – Enfield do seem to think of everything to make this park as accessible as possible to as many of us as possible. Follow the rail, keeping it to your left, until you see an obelisk ahead, then step over the rail to the left and go through scrub and across grassland parallel to the road which runs through the park. Watch for traffic. If you want to visit the loos, information centre or cafe they are to the right, along the road. The cafe has tables outside at which your dog can sit with you. Nearby is a picnic area where, for a small fee, you can have a barbecue.

To continue on the main walk

Turn left on the approach road, put your dog on the lead, go through the gateway and cross Cockfosters Road (there's no crossing and the road is busy, so you may have to make a run for it). Turn right and in a few metres, go left down Chalk Lane. Almost immediately bear right on Games Road, following a Pymmes Brook waymark. Go through a white gate and – if you can trust your dog near the very occasional, slow-moving car – release him in the scrub to the right and follow the rough path downhill. Games Road peters out and the path joins a wider track with another Pymmes Brook waymark. Descend the gentle slope and see Arundel Road parallel to your walk on the left. It isn't fenced but it's far enough away to be fairly safe – besides what dog would want to rush onto a road when he has woods to explore? At the bottom of the next slope cross a brick bridge over – you've guessed it – Pymmes Brook. Immediately after the bridge is a wooden signpost. To the left it points along the Pymmes Brook Trail. If you want to follow it you can; and find your way back to

Fed up with entire world — and with each other.

Oakhill Park. If your dog is in need of a drink, the bank slopes gently to the right, so he can easily wade into the brook.

Meanwhile I read, with horror, the legend on the arm of the signpost which pointed straight ahead. 'Barnet two miles.' I looked southwest. The sun was a great red-orange ball about to slip below the horizon. I checked my watch. It was 3.17pm and the date was 9 December. Back at Trent Park I'd noticed the closing time – sunset – was 4pm. Could I make it to Barnet before then? I was going to have to try. I set off at somewhere between a frenzied walk and a run. If you are there on a winter afternoon you will plunge into a chill, low-lying mist in the valley. A cyclist pedalled past but there was no one else. The path becomes a track and the track becomes a road. It crosses the railway via a white bridge. On the other side continue straight on the footpath beside the white six-bar gate. You are on Bakers Hill, a quiet road leading only to the open space you have just left. What is the open space? It's Monken Hadley Common and if you turn you will see a sign to confirm this. On it read, 'Take nothing but photographs. Leave nothing but footprints. No fires. No horseriding. No vehicles. No motor cycles.' Months later I returned to the common on a bright spring day and found acres of woodland and scrub in which Fred had a whale of a time. So if you want freedom for your dog on a summer weekend when your local park is packed with people, then this is the place to come.

To reach New Barnet BR

Take the track to the left of the road and follow the footpath south alongside Tudor Golf Course. Keep going all the way to Station Road. Cross it by Triangle Passage and go straight ahead to reach the station.

To continue on the main route

Cross the next rough footbridge to your right, cross the bridge onto the common. Turn left and follow the path parallel to Bakers Hill. The undergrowth to the right should be intriguing enough to keep your dog away from the road. At the top of the hill, the path rejoins the road at the junction with Hadley Road and it's time to put your dog on the lead. Turn left through the gate into Hadley Road. Walk down it with north London's suburbs spread out below you. At

Tudor Road – the second turning – turn right beside the Hadley Hotel which has an old red telephone box in its garden. When you reach a path to the right turn into it, release your dog. You are in King George's Field.

King George's Field isn't just one field. It's a network of rough open, hilly spaces linked by paths and occasionally running along-side allotments. After the brick building inside the entrance, release your dog and turn left across the grass beside back gardens. Pass through an iron gate and turn left, then left into another field and left almost immediately through a gap in the hedge. Put your dog on the lead to walk a few paces along the quiet street, then right down steps. At the bottom turn right along Norfolk Road. More playing fields – private ones – are to your right. The road curves and becomes a footpath called Burnside Close. At its end turn right on Meadway and go straight up the hill. At the top, turn left, follow the signs for High Barnet tube and descend the footpath to the station.

To reach the Finchley walks

At the top of Meadway, cross Barnet Hill at the lights and turn left. There is a hilly, green space to your right and a path leading down into it, plus red bins for dog waste. You are free to release your dog here, but I didn't – the traffic on Barnet Hill moves far too fast for my liking. Follow the path through the green space to Underhill. With your dog on the lead cross the road and go straight ahead into Barnet Lane. Take the next left (Westcombe Drive) and the next right (Fairfield Way). Continue along Fairfield Way until it becomes Grosvenor Avenue. Shortly thereafter, to your right is the entrance to a public playing field. Go into it and release your dog. There are plenty of dog mess bins here.

Turn left along the tarmac path and – if your dog is anything like Fred – distract him with titbits or with his own ball from the umpteen ball games – cricket is the main one – going on around you. At Western Avenue the path joins the route of the Dollis south. The fields beside it are full of wild flowers. We left the path at Fursby Avenue, turned left and climbed the short, gentle incline, turned left again and found West Finchley tube. It's above ground, so no lifts escalators, only a bridge to cross for southbound trains.

Walk 15: Oval to Balham

High spots – in the literal as well as the figurative sense – are One Tree Hill and Sydenham Hill Wood. These pockets of secluded 'countryside' are a startling contrast to the blighted acres of Burgess Park. Be prepared for some very steep hills and, if you are white, the salutary experience of being in a minority. Connects with Walk 20.

Route: Oval to Balham with short diversions to Peckham Rye BR, Nunhead BR, Honor Oak BR, Forest Hill BR, Sydenham BR, Sydenham Hill BR, Crystal Palace BR, Gypsy Hill BR, West Norwood BR and Streatham BR; longer diversions to West Dulwich BR, North Dulwich BR and Denmark Hill BR.

Distance: 14 miles

Facilities: Loos in Kennington Park, Brenchley Gardens, Horniman Gardens, Crystal Palace Park, Norwood Park, Tooting Common. Cafes in Kennington Park, Horniman Gardens, Crystal Palace Park, Tooting Common. Pubs along the route.

Oval Station has a spiral staircase (follow the sign to the emergency stairs). Cross Harleyford Street, then Kennington Park Road and Brixton Road to enter Kennington Park to the left and release your dog. Take the path straight ahead. After the cafe take the left fork and put your dog on the lead. Turn right on Agnes Place. There are lived-in buses here – with swirls of bright paint on their exteriors. In a few paces enter an open space to your left and release your dog. Walk straight across the grass to a tarmac path and turn left. At the barrier put your dog on the lead and continue on the path to pass under the arch through Molesworth House (a block of flats) and follow Maddock Way past steel-grilled shops to Cook's Road. Turn right, cross Hillingdon Road and continue along Dale's Road to turn left at John Ruskin Street.

At Camberwell Road turn right. We came across a wino sitting on a bench. Turn left after him into Burgess Park and release your dog.

Burgess Park was made by the GLC along the route of the former Grand Surrey Canal. This part of Southwark is seriously lacking in greenery and people certainly seem to enjoy walking their dogs across the extensive rough grass. But Burgess Park is, frankly, peculiar. It's peculiar because it's so obviously artificial. It's peculiar because of the faded grandeur of some of the adjacent buildings which stick out like sore thumbs in the urban grime. And it's peculiar because of the glossy, two-sided, full colour leaflet which the council has produced about it, for all the world as though the park had the pulling power of Buck House or Madame Tussauds. Incidentally, poop scooping in Southwark is a voluntary affair, but there are plans to make it compulsory.

Burgess Park is primarily open grassland, but at its north eastern tip is its most extraordinary feature: the Burgess Park lake. Concrete walk-ways surround its deep, choppy waters and beyond to the west is a vista of high rise blocks. The entire scene is decidedly eerie and has none of the natural contours and soft plantings of shrubs which edge the charming lake in Victoria park in the similarly deprived borough of Hackney (see Walk 19).

Go straight ahead to pass an old brick kiln and under the Wells Way underpass to a dirty paved area which Southwark Council calls 'The Plaza'. Take the right hand path and follow it all the way to the end of the park to exit by a gate onto St. George's Way. Put your dog on the lead. There is a green sign on the railing urging people not to vandalise their environment. Just behind you is a scrapyard with high, battered walls, behind which resounded ominous bangings and clankings. Turn left, left again into Trafalgar Avenue, cross the road, enter the Surrey Canal Linear Park straight in front of you and release your dog. This park (and Burgess Park) are on the route of a proposed Green Chain through Southwark. The plan is that it will extend north east to Southwark Park, Russia Dock Woodland and Stave Hill Ecological Park (where the photo on the cover of this book was taken) – but at the moment those northern open spaces are green islands in a sea of urban streets.

Back in the Surrey Canal Linear Park follow the path along the course of the old canal under the red brick bridges which used to span the water. It is securely fenced all the way – apart from paths which run into it from neighbouring streets. When you enter a

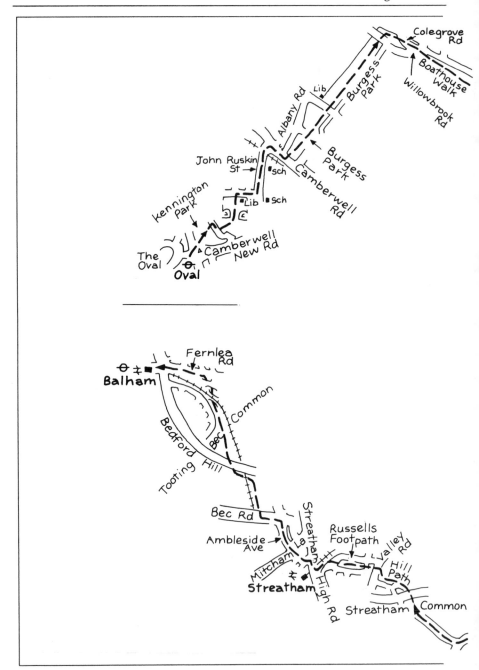

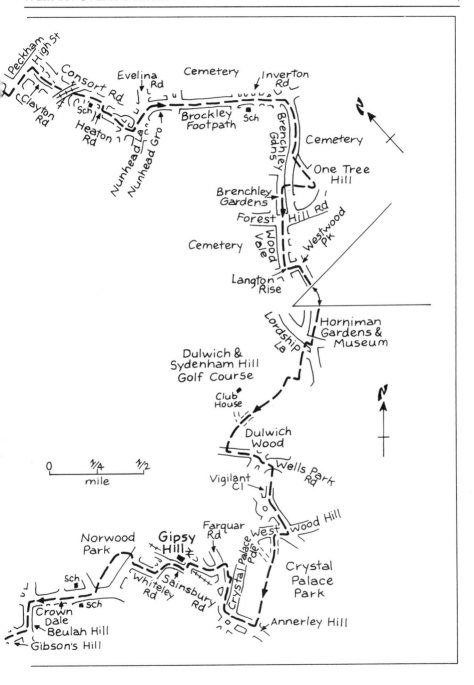

roofed, paved area, put your dog on the lead. Go down the steps, turn right on Peckham High Street, cross it at the lights, then cross Rye Lane to your left and walk straight along Peckham High Street's narrow pavement. Cross Clayton Road, turn right along it, take any of the entrances to the gardens of the housing estate to your left and, keeping your dog on the lead of course, walk the length of the path between grass to emerge at the junction of Clayton Road and Consort Road. Cross Clayton Road and keep straight under the railway bridge. Peckham Rye BR is to your right. Cross Heaton Road, take a few steps along it and turn left into Manaton Close. You are again in the gardens of a housing estate, so don't release your dog or let him foul the grass. Turn right on Philip Walk, left at Galatea Square and right and left again in Old James Street. Turn left on Nunhead Lane.

If you turn right instead of left you reach Peckham Rye Park and Common which together make up one of Southwark's largest open spaces. I didn't because I'd been there before and both Fred and I found this flat, closely-mown 39 hectare expanse pretty dull. However there is a nice pub on the junction of Peckham Rye and Barry Road. The landlord has a dog himself and is quite happy for your mutt to sit inside the bar in the warm, which is rare these days. He also has an intriguing collection of antique clocks.

Assuming you've turned left on Nunhead Lane, take the next right (Linden Grove).

To reach Nunhead BR

At the end of Linden Grove, turn left into Oakdale and right into Gibbon Road to find the station.

To continue on the main route

As the road curves by the Belvedere pub, follow the sign pointing to the right along Brockley Footpath and release your dog. On your left is Nunhead Cemetery, on your right water works. Both have high fences. The path is extremely steep. From the summit descend the southern slope to Dorland Road, put your dog on the lead and go straight ahead along Inverton Road, then Mertins Road and right into Brenchley Gardens. At the junction stand the remains of an old brick railway bridge. There is greenery on both sides of Brenchley Gardens but unfortunately you can't go into it with your dog.

After Camberwell New Cemetery on the left is One Tree Hill, a delectable fragment of countryside. Inside its gate release your dog and go up the steep path between gnarled trees. At the summit, turn right. Walk straight ahead above the countrified-looking church to the oak tree which lives inside a circle of iron railing. This isn't the oak after which the hill is named – that was struck by lightning in the 1880s and a substitute planted. The original tree had many legends attached to it. The Romans are said to have defeated Boudicca after sussing out the position of her army from beside it. Queen Elizabeth I is supposed to have rested beneath its boughs. In case you're wondering about the 'One Tree' bit, the oak stood in isolation until the nineteenth century. Now there is secondary woodland all around.

Through the branches and above the church you can see miles across south London, which isn't surprising as the hill is 90 metres above sea level. I found an unvandalised bench at the far end of the summit and shared a ham sandwich and a hard boiled egg with Fred. London was spread out below me; I picked out Telecom tower, silvery in the spring sun, with black hills in the distance behind it. I'm not the only one to think this a lovely spot. John Betjeman called it, 'the nearest and strangest piece of country surviving in London,' and thought the view, 'better than that from Parliament Hill on Hampstead Heath.'

To reach Honor Oak BR

Go down the southern slope of the hill on the path past the church to the gate onto Honor Oak Park and turn left to reach the station.

To continue on the main route

Follow the path down the northern slope through trees. At the gate put your dog on the lead, cross the road and go through the gate into Brenchley Gardens. Release your dog – there is a high railing between him and the traffic. The gardens are on the embankment of the old Crystal Palace Railway line which closed in 1954. The remains of the bridge on Mertins Road were part of this railway too. The nearest part of the gardens are formal, but the embankment, to your right, is wild and the undergrowth harbours squirrels. Walk parallel to the road, keeping to the right of two stone urns swathed in stone cloth. Put your dog on the lead, cross Forest Hill Road and go straight along Wood Vale beside Camberwell Old Cemetery. Turn left at Langton Rise and right on Westwood Park.

When the road bends left, take the footpath to the right between Numbers 43 and 45. Release your dog. To your left is Horniman Gardens which houses the Horniman Museum full of artefacts which Frederick Horniman (of Horniman's tea fame) collected from all over the world. Keep straight along the path and when you see Lordship Lane ahead put your dog on the lead.

To reach Forest Hill BR

Turn left along London Road, left on Devonshire Road and follow it to the station.

To reach North Dulwich BR

Turn left on Lordship Lane, then left on Dulwich Common. Enter Dulwich Park at Rosebery Lodge, release your dog and follow the track to the left which curves to exit at Court Lane Gate. Put your dog on the lead, turn left along Court Lane, then follow Dulwich village to the right, cross Village Way into Red Post Hill and find the station to your right.

To reach Denmark Hill BR

At the end of Court Street turn right up Calton Avenue which merges with Townley Road to take you left to cross East Dulwich Grove. Go up Greendale which becomes a path between playing fields on which you can release your dog. As you approach Wanley Road replace the lead. Turn right, left into Arnold Avenue, right into Champion Hill, next left and right on Denmark Hill and right on Champion Park to find the station.

To continue on the main route

Cross Lordship Lane by the traffic lights and, directly opposite the path you have just left, find Lapse Wood Walk which used to lead to now-demolished Lordship Lane station. Keep your dog on the lead to cross a service road. Follow a the line of street lamps across a second road and up a grassy hill. Watch for a gap in the fence to your right, step inside it and release your dog.

You are in Sydenham Hill Wood. Together with Dulwich Wood its trees cover 25 hectares. But although the wood looks like the countryside it is a nature reserve run by the London Wildlife Trust. Dogs are allowed to run free, but they should be under close control which Mathew Frith, the Wood's warden, says means no mad rushing through the undergrowth. He asked me to think too – which I hadn't before – of the effect of dog mess on the Wood's ecology. Too much of it could change the composition of the soil which in turn could mean changes in the kinds of plants which grow here. So use your plastic bags.

Turn right and go down the slope to the footbridge. Brick piers carry the bridge across a cutting which was once part of – you've guessed it – the old railway line to Crystal Palace. The bridge was built to carry a bridleway called Cox's walk. In 1871 the French Impressionist painter Pissaro sat here and painted a picture which now hangs in the Courtauld gallery. The station he painted has gone and so has the original bridge – this one's a replica built in 1908. On the opposite bank go into the first of two green gates to the left. Take the second path which will soon run parallel to a golf course, then allotments.

The wood is a remnant of the Great North Wood which once covered the high ridge of land stretching from Deptford to Selhurst. The Great North Wood itself was a descendant of the same 'wildwood' that I crossed in Walk 1. The story of its destruction is much the same as in north London. While the wood was needed it was coppiced to keep supplies regular. But by the early nineteenth century London was expanding and the switch from wood to coal for heating made timber much less valuable. Only a few fragments, of which Sydenham Hill Wood is one, were saved from development.

In 1854 the Crystal Palace was relocated from Hyde Park after the Great Exhibition. The area became fashionable and large villas were built on Sydenham Hill. Luckily the Victorians were fond of woodland gardens so they left many trees standing and planted other species around them. In 1865 the railway whose track-bed is such a feature of this walk was built. In 1911 98 trains a day ran along the line; but a decade later the Palace was in decline and the railway had few passengers. Later, the villas became derelict and nature recolonised their gardens.

Pass the pretty pond which is home to dragonflies, newts and frogs. Don't let your dog disturb them. At the next junction turn left and at a gate in an iron railing put your dog on the lead and turn left up steep Low Cross Lane.

To reach Sydenham Hill BR

Turn right along the lane and left on College Road.

To continue on the main route

At the top of the lane is Dulwich Wood House which is a listed building built around 1840. It has a white belvedere. It's also a pub with a beer garden and serves food. Afterwards, turn right on Crescent Wood Road, cross Sydenham Hill and go straight along Wells Road. Watch for a gap in the fence to the right next to a brick building, go through it, down steps, through the gate to your right and release your dog. Follow the twisty path with iron railings on either side. And – guess what? – we are on the course of the old railway line again. Look behind to see a bricked up bridge. The spot on which you are standing is the site of Upper Sydenham Station, the brick building you passed was the booking hall.

Cross a grassy open space, turn the corner into Vigilante Close, put your dog on the lead, turn left and walk up steep High Level Drive. Cross Westwood Hill, turn right, step inside the entrance to Crystal Palace Park to your left and release your dog. This is a poop scoop park and the penalty for not cleaning up after your dog is £200. You are in Bromley and musn't let your dog foul the pavement, verge, *or gutter*. Follow the path downhill past loos and turn right along the broad carriageway. There is lots to explore in Crystal Palace Park. It contains a children's zoo, the National Sport Centre Stadium, a boating lake and the strange prehistoric monsters built in 1853 under the guidance of Professor Richard Owen, inventor of the word 'dinosaur'. And of course the Park used to contain the Palace, a huge building constructed of glass and cast iron. The palace burned to the ground in 1936 in a blaze which could be seen from Brighton. Nothing remains except the terraces to the right of the road on which you are walking. The radio mast rears above them. This part of the route has a similar feel to Alexandra Park (see Walk 1) – it retains some sense of grandeur in its wrought iron railings and ornate gates, but it seems to have lost its heart. Put your dog on the lead to cross the car park and the access road beyond.

To reach Crystal Palace BR

Turn left along the access road to Crystal Palace Station Road.

To continue on the main route

Turn right on Anerley Hill and at the roundabout cross Crystal Palace Road. There are take-away cafes here. Go along Crystal Palace Road, left on Farquhar Road, right on steep Bowley Lane and stop. Step inside the open gate to your left and release your dog. You have entered another fragment of the Great North Wood, the delightful and rather odd Dulwich Upper Wood. Follow the path straight ahead past a visitor centre and an information board. The wood is a 5 acre (2 hectare) nature reserve managed by the Trust for Urban Ecology. Like Sydenham Hill Wood it once held Victorian villas. You'll pass foundations and even a brick hearth nestling incongruously in a bank. Do remember that the entire site is a nature reserve and don't let your dog run riot. When the path rejoins Farquhar Road put him on the lead and go straight ahead into Dulwich Wood Avenue. Take the first left into Colby Road, left into Gypsy Hill and Gypsy Hill BR is in front of you. Cross to the station, turn left and sharp right into Sainsbury Road. There is no pavement on either side of it, so watch out for traffic. The road curves left to become Bristow Road in which the front gardens sport wrecked cars and piles of junk. A small, black mongrel dozed on a mound of rags. A soap box cart hurtled down the hill with an old banger weaving inches behind it.

At the top of the road turn right into Whiteley Road, cross Salters Hill, turn right, enter Norwood Park and release your dog. The park used to be a common with the lost river Effra running along one edge. Now it is dull. Climb the hill and go to the right of the fenced paddling pool.

To reach West Norwood BR

Go straight down the path with toilets to your right and a fenced
hard play area at the bottom to the left. At Elder Road put your dog
on the lead and turn right to find the station.

To continue on the main route

Take the next path left beside the extraordinarily large picnic area
(into which dogs aren't allowed) to reach the junction of Elder Road,
Central Hill and Crown Dale. With your dog on the lead cross Crown
Dale and turn right. There's a private school to your left with
extensive green grounds. You are in Croydon. Signs warn you not
to allow your dog to foul the pavement or the grass verge. What grass
verge? In a few moments we came to some squares of bare earth in
which daffodils were making a blighted effort to grow. At the top of
the hill the last square had sprouted something else: a rusty, white
mini.

Turn left at Beulah Hill, right into Gibson's Road – and enter
another world. The street is lined with flowering cherries and every
driveway holds a shiny car or two. At the second junction step inside
the gate of Norwood Grove, release your dog and turn right along
the path. Ahead is a white mansion, to the left a green swathe of
parkland. Just before the mansion, turn right along the path behind
the house to pass a red brick lodge and enter Streatham Common.
Follow the path across grassland to the car park, cross its right-hand
edge and another path and head straight across the grass to an old
iron bollard on Streatham Common North (a main road).

Cross, go straight ahead into Hill Path and release your dog. You're
in graffiti-land again – the corrugated iron fence at the first bend is
covered in it. The path is securely fenced. At Valley Road put your
dog on the lead and turn right. Two kids on one pushbike were
chasing the white line in the middle of the road while cars rushed
past in both directions. I held my breath for them.

Cross the road to find Russell's Path. Its sign may be thickly
defaced. Release your dog in this drab lane running between high
fences made of everything from breeze blocks to corrugated iron.
Watch out for gaps through which he might squeeze. Put him on the
lead to cross Madeira Road and keep him on it for the short

Fred warned me of what was to come by dashing ahead and sinking up to his tum.

remaining stretch of path which leads to Streatham High Road. Streatham BR is in front of you.

Turn right, left into Gleneagles Road, right into Ambleside Avenue and cross Mitcham Lane, then cross Tooting Bec Road and turn left along the edge of the common. Just before the railway bridge take a path down steps past a yellow waymark through woods to your right and release your dog. Tooting Bec Common is 220 acres (88 hectares) of grassland and woodland. It is managed by the London Borough of Wandsworth. Remember their policy on dogs from Walk 12? You don't need to pick up after your dog on this route, but much of the rest of the Common is a poop scoop area and there are some spots – the nature reserve round the lake for one – where no dogs are allowed. So if you want to wander, check your free Wandsworth poop scoop map first.

You are walking through Streatham Woods. At Bedford Hill, turn left, cross the railway, cross the road to the right and, just after the colourful sign for Balham, take the path to the right. If you don't turn right you can press along Bedford Hill (with your dog on the lead) and join the southwards trail to Tea House Wood (where, yes, there is a tea house). Instead we carried on north through Bedford Hill Woods.

Emerge in the open grassland of Bedford Hill Field where, according to Wandsworth Council,' the ground is wetter as it is clayey and low-lying.' They weren't joking. I'd already given up hope of my new white trainers returning from the day in the condition they started out – but this was something else. Luckily Fred warned me of what was to come by dashing ahead and sinking up to his tum. I turned left across the grass towards a tarmac path (Culverden Path). Follow it under two bridges, put your dog on the lead and turn left on Fernlea road across Bedford Hill to Balham tube. It has fixed stairs as well as escalators. Fred fell asleep the instant we were on the train and I made a good show of ignoring all the clean, dressed-up people setting out for a Saturday night in the West End.

Walk 16: Dagenham East circular

A tour of The Chase Nature Reserve beside the River Rom: a watery, deserted landscape with horses grazing on unfenced land and lots of wildfowl.

Route: Dagenham East circular walk

Distance: 3½ miles

Facilities: None

Dagenham East has stairs. Cross Rainham Road and turn right. Ignore the lane ahead of you which leads between heaps of serious rubbish (bedsteads, old tyres etc.) into a tangled scrap of woodland with the rotting branches of trees obscuring every attempt at a path and the rotting corpse of an urban fox. Continue along Rainham Road to turn left on Western Avenue. Walk past the school, take the next left and at the end of the street follow the green footpath sign to the right. Release your dog. There is a large, securely fenced lake to your left. To your right are the ends of long, straight, gardens, some of which are not securely fenced – and one of which harbours a vociferous Doberman. After the lake take the path to the left. Watch for tethered horses grazing on the scrubby ground. Keep following the path up and down the gullies to cross the Central Line by the footbridge. Turn right along a fenced green path to hop over the wooden stile ahead. There are small ponds to your left with stubby beige reeds poking from the water. You are in the Chase Nature Reserve which covers 120 acres (48 hectares). There are no restrictions on dogs (though they musn't chase the horses or the wild birds).

How did the Chase come about? Until the beginning of this century it was still small farms. In the 1920s and 30s it became gravel works: the gravel was used to build houses. In the 1970s some of the gravel pits were filled with rubble, but others were left and are now

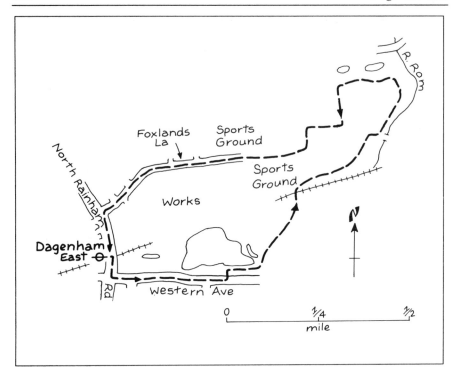

full of water – havens for waterfowl, a pleasure to the eye and a boon
for a very thirsty Fred. The Chase is Green Belt and is part of the
Dagenham Corridor along which you can walk, as you can along so
many green strips radiating from the city, clear out of London and
– in this case – into Essex.

But we're taking a more modest trip. Follow the path as it bends
left. Cross a narrow plank bridge over a ditch. Watch out for horse
manure in which your dog may roll. Ahead is a rabbit warren. The
track leads to the right and brings you out in a wide, green area, with
more water to your left. I watched a black labrador splashing
joyously; he was the only dog I saw on the entire trip.

When you join a parallel track, the river Rom is across the grass
to your right. Ahead in the distance was an elderly chestnut horse
standing stock still, nodding its head in the sun. Beside us, suddenly,
were two horses with riders approaching at a smart trot. The riders
thanked me for holding Fred while they passed. Carry on along the

The riders thanked me for holding Fred.

track leading away from the Rom to the left and towards a swampy area. Fenced, private paddocks are to your right with a riding stable beyond. There is a large pond between you and the paddocks and a notice to the left on which I read, 'Wildfowl Area, please keep out.' Make sure your dog observes this rule. Go straight ahead up a shallow slope to lots of funny little green tumps. Left again and you join a wide green track. The wildfowl area (it's called the Slack) is now to your left. Teal, Shoveler, Grey Heron, Common Tern, Lapwing and Snipe live among the reeds there.

Climb a stile to the right into a fenced area. Behind us a cavalry of horses from the riding stable spilled out onto the grass and began circling nose to tail. Take the shingle path to a kissing gate and follow a sign pointing to, 'Public Footpath to Dagenham Road and to Rainham Road South' beside the railway. Your path turns into a concrete track called Foxlands Lane and brings you back to Rainham Road on which you should turn left to reach the tube.

Walk 17: Wembley Park circular

Worth a whole day out to enjoy the waterside walks of the Welsh Harp Open Space and the unique medieval meadows of Fryent Country Park. Very little road walking. Connects with Walk 5.

Route: Wembley Park circular walk with a diversion to Brent Cross.

Distance: 5½ miles

Facilities: Loos and cafes at Brent Cross – but a picnic in the meadows is a much better option.

Outside Wembley Park, which has fixed stairs, turn right, left on Chalkhill Road, then right on Windsor Crescent. Just before the Crescent rejoins the road take the footpath to the right which leads across a pleasant grassy stretch behind a housing estate with the tube line to your right – and release your dog. Be sure to pick up after him. At a narrow, quiet road, put him on the lead and cross to enter the recreation ground directly opposite. Turn left, climb through the hole in the gate and a few metres further take the tarmac lane to the right, then a tarmac path half right and release your dog. There is greenery on either side.

Go left over the bridge and turn left on the path to curve around a housing estate and reach Quainton Street Nature Reserve – a wild, green stretch beside the Brent. Go past the pond, through woodland, then across grass to put your dog on the lead at busy Blackbird Hill. Cross it, turn left, then right on Birchen Grove, walk its length to the Welsh Harp Open Space and release your dog. The Open Space spreads over 170 acres (68 hectares). Take the right fork in the path – and soon you will see the huge reservoir, its clear waters glinting in the sun. The reservoir is owned by the British Waterways Board, but it isn't at all your average reservoir. It was opened in 1835, not to supply drinking water but to feed the Grand Union Canal System. It isn't fenced but instead is fringed with luscious wetlands through which you can walk – and has natural, sloping banks. Sailing, windsurfing and canoeing are the main pursuits here; they're a treat to watch – bright sails gliding across the clear, blue water. There's

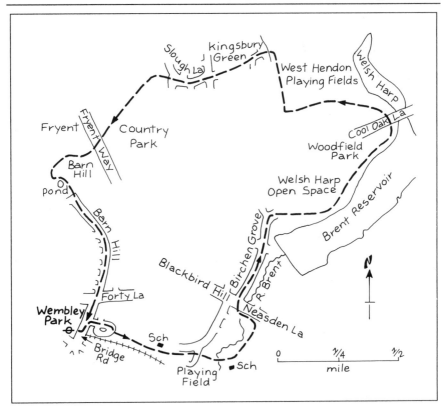

plenty of fun for your dog too. Continue on the path through grassland and you will find several shallow beaches where he can have a drink and a swim. Watch out for places where the ground is marshy or the water deep. The path narrows, runs between trees, then climbs a hill to emerge on Cool Oak Lane.

To reach Brent Cross

Do not attempt to do so if you are as scared of heights as I am. The things which look like footbridges on the A to Z are in fact a labyrinth of terrifying narrow walk-ways over umpteen lanes of speeding traffic.

Turn right on Cool Oak Lane with your dog on the lead, take the path to the right on the other side of a car park and follow it to reach Priestley Way (parts of this path are only open in the summer). Turn

. . . terrifying narrow walk-ways over umpteen lanes of speeding traffic.

left, go under the flyover and be prepared not to enjoy the rest of the trip one bit. It's filthy as well as scary. Turn right, go under a railway bridge, climb the frightening footbridge to a follow a path across a huge traffic island. Take the next footbridge to the left. Fred was nonchalant about these footbridges – I was gripping the handrail in white-knuckled terror with one hand and his lead in the other. Descend – thank goodness! – to a slip road leading to the vast Brent Cross Car Park. Go straight ahead to cross the river Brent, which here is a sluggish channel so dirty it looks more like an open sewer than the charming waterway in Walk 5. Its shallow trickle harbours rusting shopping trolleys and quantities of litter.

Turn right on Prince Charles Drive past the Shopping Centre and follow the signs along paths, across a small area of grubby grass over the North Circular and under several flyovers to reach Heathfield Gardens (a street) and the station. It has stairs.

To continue on the main route

Put your dog on the lead, cross Cool Oak Lane and release him again beside the Youth Sailing Base to follow the wild path beside the water. Between April and July make sure your dog does not disturb birds in the breeding areas – there are signs to warn you where these are. Follow the next distinct path left beside allotments to reach the southern tip of West Hendon Playing Fields. Unusually, dogs are permitted on the fields, although they are of course a poop scoop area. Skirt the football pitches, keeping them to your right, allowing your dog to enjoy the scrub beside them and when you reach the end of the fields turn right to take the approach road to the left between a Scout hut and a football ground. Turn right across the mown expanse of Silver Jubilee Park parallel to Townend Lane. When you see a fenced children's play area to your left, put your dog on the lead, cross Townend Road and take Elthorne Way to reach a recreation ground – it's a poop scoop park in which you can release your dog. After a few steps on the tarmac path, strike across the grass half left, aiming to reach the other side just above the football pitches. There you will exit the recreation ground by a tarmac lane beside a children's play area. Put your dog on the lead, cross Church Lane (there's a pub with tables outside at the junction) and go along Plough Lane. Cross Salmon Street and enter Fryent Country Park by the green lane ahead. Don't release your dog yet, there are fields of horses on either side. At the end of the paddocks let your dog free – and enjoy the rolling meadows.

Fryent Country Park is seriously beautiful, remarkably secluded, delightfully large (252 acres, 100 hectares) and has no restrictions on dogs. Oddly, there are few of them about. We visited the park on a mild autumn Sunday afternoon and met only a handful of people and their mutts strolling across the long grass under a still-warm but fading sun.

If you are in a hurry go straight ahead with the hedgerow of Home Field to your right, press on across two more meadows (Goldringe and Richards east), then turn left into Mead and right to put your dog on the lead well before the speeding traffic of Fryent Way. I daresay you will have to wait several minutes before you can safely cross – there is no crossing to link the two sections of the park.

But the park deserves a much more leisurely tour. To take in the best of its views and its variety of terrain (and to give your dog a good run) turn right at the end of the paddocks. If you don't trust your dog near horses, keep to the meadow to the left. Pass three ponds to your right (they were dry when we were there). There are 15 ponds in the park, many of which are a legacy of the time when every field had its own pond. At the access path to Slough Lane turn sharp left to reach the wide open space of Gotfords Hill and take the trodden path across it to the south. The hill is yet another meadow, is 63 metres above sea level and from it you can see St. Mary's church on the summit of Harrow's Hill. But that is not its main attraction. In front of you, in spite of the proximity of Brent Cross and the traffic of Fryent Way, there is no visible indication that you are in London. The green slope stretches gently to meet a cloud-streaked sky and to your right are densely wooded hills. In summer the meadows are thick with wild flowers – in autumn there are blackberries and sloes in the hedges. Some of the hedges in the park are newly restored – and some are home to field voles. Watch your dog doesn't chase these little creatures; I spotted one and sang out, 'Leave!' just in time.

The meadows in the park are now called by the names shown in a map of 1597, though there is nothing on the ground to indicate this. Brent Council manages the park for wildlife and conservation, but has erected no obtrusive signs to tell you what you see. For more information you should phone their ecology unit (you may be lucky enough to speak to Cathy Rose who is an enthusiastic dog owner herself) on 0181 296 0492. The rangers from the unit in conjunction with Wembley & District Canine Society run the Barham Park Dog Show as part of their efforts to promote responsible ownership.

From Gotfords Hill cross Goldringe, Richards east and Meade to reach Fryent Way and put your dog on the lead. Or, if you have time, wander south through Dormers Meade and Great Hillcroach to find the path south again, through scrub, beside the back gardens of the houses on Salmon Way. I expect it will be deserted. After this lovely diversion turn right before you hit Fryent Way and go back through Dormers Meade to cross the road to the left.

You are in a car park – there are unlikely to be many cars there – with an information board to your right. If you want you can turn right along Hell Lane. It's an ancient trackway that had fallen into disuse as early as 1619. It will lead you to Richards west (another meadow), from which you can branch off to the left through more fields to follow a scrub-lined track beside the Jubilee line and find the Gaderbrook, which is a tributary of the Wealdstone Brook.

From thence take a broad circle round to the left (your dog will love it) to reach the base of the woods leading to Barn Hill. Take any upward track to gain the summit. If your dog enjoys jumping as much as Fred does, then there are lots of fallen logs in the wood for him to leap over.

Alternatively, from the car park, release your dog and press straight ahead across a grassy patch (Fred enjoyed a game of ball here) into woodland. Take the right fork. Appreciate the view of north London's trees to your right. At a large fallen log (Fred jumped it), turn left uphill along a path. It becomes a wide, green ride. The woods were planted in 1793 by landscape architect Humphrey Repton. At the top is a round fish pond and beyond a grassy space with a white triangulation point, used as a marker by map makers earlier this century. Green rides lead to right and left – contrived pathways which contrast oddly with the natural simplicity of the rest of Fryent Country Park. Don't take either ride, but press on across the grass to put your dog on the lead, say goodbye to Fryent Park until another day, walk straight down Barn Hill, cross Forty Avenue to go along Bridge Road and return to the station.

Walk 18: Willesden Junction circular

Railways, the Grand Union Canal and the deliciously wild open space of Wormwood Scrubs Park. The complete circuit involves quite a bit of road walking, but if you go on a weekend, the streets are likely to be deserted. Connects with Walk 5.

Route: Willesden Junction circular walk passing Acton Main Line BR, West Acton and Park Royal; access to East Acton and North Action and extension walks to Kensal Green, Kensal Rise BR, White City and Shepherd's Bush.

Distance: 7½ miles

Facilities: Pubs en route – several beside the canal have gardens. Open air snack bar in North Acton Recreation Ground.

Exit Willesden station (it has stairs), turn right on Station Approach, then left on Old Oak Lane. Cross the canal, take the path to the left and release your dog. This is the Paddington Arm of the Grand Union The tow-path here is narrow and neatly mown. To your right, securely fenced, is a vast complex of railway interchanges. This is a favourite place for trainspotters – we came across two in anoraks perched on a bench, peering over the wall through binoculars. Pass under a blue bridge and at the next bridge, which is red, put your dog on the lead and follow the path to the right.

To reach Kensal Green or Kensal Rise BR

Stay on the tow-path. This stretch from Mitre Bridge (the bridge under which you have just passed) is very green, with the trees of St. Mary's and Kensal Green cemeteries on the other bank.

Fred kept teetering on the edge of the water peering at the families of ducks; and I kept telling him, 'Leave!' So far he'd obeyed, but now he looked over his shoulder with an expression which obviously said, 'I've been swimming umpteen times in the dog pond on Hampstead Heath and I know what this business is about,' and

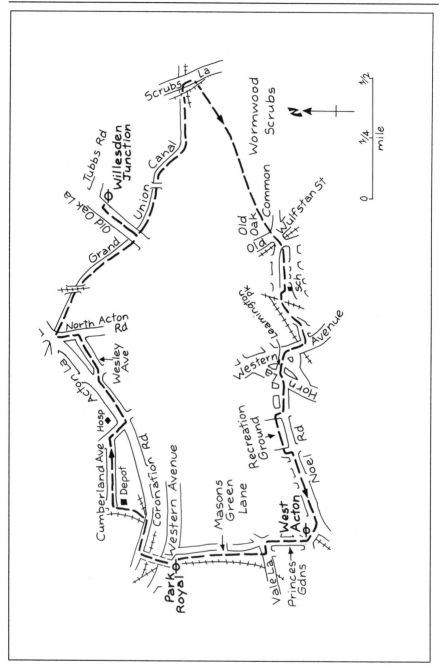

This is a favourite place for trainspotters.

plunged in. He was instantly out of his depth. I pulled him out and he ran along in a damp, embarrassed fashion, clearly hoping that no one else had seen him make such a fool of himself. Pass grey gasholders to the right and a picnic area with a foetid pool and three tables. An old man in black with no shoes sat at one of them.

At a Sainsburys superstore on the waterfront with narrow boats moored beside it put your dog on the lead and turn left along Ladbroke Grove. Kensal Green and Kensal Rise BR are both about ten minutes walk away. To reach the first, turn left on Harrow Road. To find the second, cross Harrow Road into Kilburn Lane, go left on Chamberlayne Road, cross Harvist Road and continue straight ahead to the station. Both stations have fixed stairs.

To continue on the main route

Turn right on Scrubs Lane, pass under the railway bridge, watch for a gap in the rustic post and rail fencing to your right, step inside and release your dog. You are in Wormwood Scrubs Park. Wormwood Scrubs isn't just a prison – the prison lies to the south of 42 hectares of open space. It is the largest open space in the borough of Hammersmith & Fulham. In the Middle Ages it was woodland and called Wormholt Wood because of the many snakes in it. By the mid-eighteenth century all the trees had been felled, so the oldest woodland in the entire park was planted by the GLC in the mid-1980s. The Scrubs was the scene of attempts at flying in the early part of the century by, among others, Claude Graham White. Nowadays it still has a special area for flying model aircraft. Cross a rough footbridge, go straight ahead and when you emerge from scrub turn right. You are in Hammersmith & Fulham and if your dog does his business in the grass you must hound the result down and pick it up and carry it for quite a long time before you find a (vandalised) bin for dog mess.

On your left is a nature reserve, on your right the fenced railway. Stick close to the railway and admire the wild flowers around you. Cross the model aircraft area on a rough path. You will see traffic ahead, running parallel to your route, along Old Wulfstan Street. Follow the informal path through the grass as it curves to the left towards a terrace of red brick houses. Head for the right end of the terrace and join the junction of Braybrook Road and Old Wulfstan Street.

To reach North Action

Put your dog on the lead and turn right along Old Wulfstan Street. Cross under the railway and, just before the next railway bridge, take the footpath to the left. It will lead you under the railway to Victoria Road. Cross the main road to find the station. It has fixed stairs.

To reach East Acton

Put your dog on the lead and turn left along Old Wulfstan Street. Turn right along Erconwald Street and find the tube just past the intersection with Henchman Street. It has fixed stairs.

To reach White City

Don't turn right on Erconwald Street. Continue along Old Wulfstan Street and turn left into Dugane Road. Keep going past the prison, cross the road to the right and opposite Hammersmith Hospital, find the footpath which crosses the railway to Bentworth Road. Turn left and walk to Terrick Street. Turn right into Terrick Street and cross the Westway by the bridge at the end of it. Go down White City Road. When it curves left, follow it. Cross Wood Lane and the station is in front of you. It has stairs.

To reach Shepherd's Bush (Hammersmith & City line)

From White City Road, turn right along Africa Road. Immediately before the junction with Loftus is the entrance to Hammersmith Park to the left. Cross Hammersmith Park to Frithville Gardens. Go straight down Frithville Gardens, turn left and Shepherd's Bush tube is to your left. It has stairs.

To reach Shepherd's Bush (Central line)

Cross Wood Lane. Cross Uxbridge Road to the south and permit your dog a brief, traffic-encircled few moments of freedom on the travesty of an open space which Shepherd's Bush Common has now become. Actually Fred and I never bother with this meagre patch – we prefer sampling the smells and sounds of Shepherd's Bush market. The station has a lift and stairs.

To continue on the main route

Put your dog on the lead, cross Old Wulfstan Street at the throated barrier, take a few steps to the right and turn left, under the railway bridge, along Oak Common Lane. As soon as you can – the bend behind you is blind – cross to the right and find, hidden and unsignposted between Brunel Road and Long Drive, a tatty looking lane. Enter it. You can release your dog here, the path is fenced on either side, with mesh wire topped by barbed wire. There are lots of vacant sites with notices warning of guard dogs. You will reach the bridge over the railway. The bridge is securely fenced too, so you can let your dog run free. When he reaches the bottom of the steps at the other side, snap on his lead and turn right. Alternatively, allow him a run around the green open space to your right (it's like a tiny meadow).

You are in a pleasant housing estate. There were lots of kids playing here on their bikes. Spotting the large A to Z under my arm, the oldest boy braked to a skidding halt.

'Where do you want to go?'

'Cotton Avenue.'

He gave me directions. I set off, but by now a whole streetful of kids were on the scene – plus a golden cocker puppy without a collar. Golden cocker pursued Fred, sniffing enthusiastically. One kid after another swooped on the pup and tried to hold him, but he wriggled free.

Eventually: 'Use this string,' instructed the boy who had given us directions. He cast a knowing glance at Fred. 'She must be having her period,' he told the others.

Curve round Perry Avenue to the approach road to Western Avenue. Turn right. Walk to the traffic lights. There's a slip road to your right. Cross it and go straight ahead. *Don't* cross the slip road and *then* cross Western Avenue. If you do you will be stuck on a miniscule traffic island and be forced to make a run for it – as Fred and I were – in the split second before the filter allows the traffic from Wales Farm Road to bear down on you. Walk along the left pavement of busy Leamington Park. Turn left at Horn Lane, cross the road to the right and go straight ahead along Noel Road.

To reach Action Main line

Don't cross Horn Lane, but continue straight along it for a few minutes. The station is on the other side of the road

To continue on the main route

At the entrance to North Action Recreation Ground turn right into the ground and release your dog. There is a snack bar to your left. Turn left alongside it to follow the tarmac path to Westfields Road. Snap on the lead and continue along Noel's Road – a pleasant, suburban road with neatly-manicured hedges, reminiscent of Hampstead Garden Suburb – to the roundabout. There's a parade of shops to your left. Cross Noel Road, using the traffic island and turn left. West acton tube is to your right. Whether you plan to go home from there or not, cross the zebra which leads to it.

If you do plan to go home, West Acton has stairs.

Take the next turn right (Princes Gardens). It has a linear garden in the middle of the road. At the next junction go right into Vale Lane and, almost immediately, opposite Monks Drive, find the entrance, to the right, to Masons Green Lane. A sign at the entrance informs you that you are now in Ealing and that the penalty for your dog fouling the lane is £50.

Release your dog. There is a secure fence to your left; insecure, gappy scrub between him and the access road to garages on your right; and ahead a green tunnel with the trees meeting above it. Plunge into it. Soon there are secure fences on both sides – the railway runs to your left behind a dense belt of scrub. On the right, as the path bends left, is high security fencing. You can now hear traffic and see Park Royal tube through the scrub to your left.

To reach Park Royal

Put your dog on the lead, descend the next sloping path to the left, cross the road (Corringway) in front of you and there's the station. It has stairs.

To continue on the main route

Don't put your dog on the lead, but do follow the path to the left – that way you'll avoid the steps. At the bottom turn sharp right and go through the subway under Western Avenue. Emerge into a small paved area and go straight ahead to cross the railway by a pleasant, cream-painted bridge. When you see Coronation Road ahead, put your dog on the lead, cross the road and turn right. The towering, brick Guinness building is to your left. Immediately after it, turn left along a footpath and release your dog. The path is securely fenced on both sides. When you reach the old-fashioned (again cream-painted) bridge over the railway, go up it to the right. At the bottom of the steps you will follow the track of the railway.

At Cumberland Avenue put your dog on the lead, follow the footpath right and emerge onto the road. I daresay this is a busy road of a weekday, it is lined with factories – but on the spring Saturday on which we visited it was deserted. At the end of Cumberland Avenue turn right into Whitby Road. At the roundabout cross to the left. Keats Restaurant, a free house with a beer garden, is to your left. Go up Acton Lane past the leafy grounds of Central Middlesex Hospital. When you spot Wesley Avenue on your right, cross the road and, ignoring Harold Road to the right, walk the length of bollarded Wesley Avenue. At the junction with North Acton Road turn left and cross Acton Lane to find a red signpost directing you left towards the path along the Grand Union Canal.

Follow the signpost, slip between the bollards to the right and release your dog. The Grand Junction Arms is on the other side of canal. From here walk straight along the tow-path to Old Oak Lane and Willesden Junction.

Walk 19: Mile End circular

Through Victoria Park – the Regent's Park of the East End – along the canal tow-path, up to the embankment on the Northern Outfall Sewer and along paths beside the area's many rivers. The walk is only for dogs who can be trusted near deep water – as Fred at long last now can – or for owners who are prepared for a shower after hauling their dogs out. Many stretches are lonely and although there is very little road walking indeed, where there is, the streets are lined with empty warehouses or scrapyards surrounded by corrugated iron. Not a walk to try on your own, but well worth following for the extraordinary industrial cityscapes through which it passes. Connects with Walk 3.

Route: Mile End circular walk passing Pudding Mill Lane DLR with diversions to Limehouse DLR, Cambridge Heath BR, Hackney Wick BR and an extension to West Ham.

Distance: 6½ miles

Facilities: Loos in and around Victoria Park. Ice cream vans and cafe in Victoria Park.

We went in a party of seven: five people, Fred and a young Rhodesian Ridgeback bitch with three times the energy of a Dalmatian; and found the walk just the right length for an early spring (though wintry cold) afternoon.

Mile End station has stairs. Turn left outside it and cross Burdett Road at the lights.

To reach Limehouse DLR

Turn left into Mile End Park and walk south along the canal, crossing roads when you come to them. When the park ends, continue on the tow-path past Salmon Lane Lock to Commercial Road Lock. Beyond the lock the canal runs into Limehouse Basin and joins the Thames. Limehouse Basin was designed by Thomas Telford and now has a marina and is headquarters to the Cruising Association. Leave the

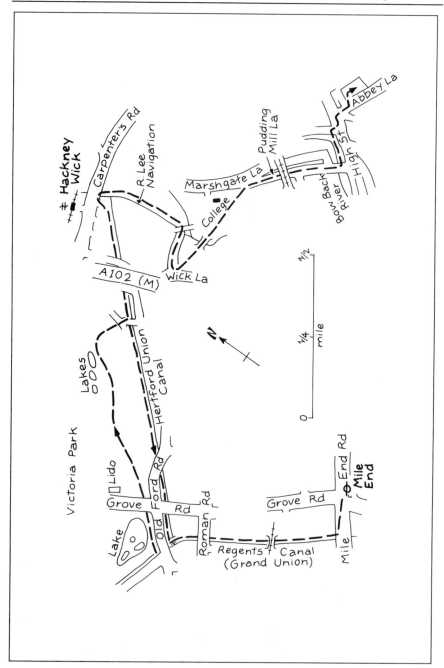

canal by the steps to the right at the lock and turn left on Commercial Road to find the station. Or you can roam around Docklands. None of the routes of the designated walks (contact the London Docklands Development Corporation on 0171 512 300 for leaflets) is likely to be green enough or vigorous enough for any dog larger than a toy, but if your mutt is small, there are newly-created parks to discover, pedestrian walk-ways a-plenty and a wealth of Dickensian associations.

To follow the main route

Cross Mile End Road to the right by the lights and find, a few steps to the right, the entrance to Mile End Park. Step inside and release your dog. Fred and Amber (the Rhodesian Ridgeback) had a wild game, barking, boxing and playing tag on the wide, fenced, grassy expanse. Follow the tarmac path which bends left to bring you to the Grand Union Canal. Step through the blue gate and turn right along the tow-path. The water looks seriously dirty, but there are signs at intervals telling you to whom to apply for a fishing permit. I don't think I'd want to fish there. If you prefer to stay in the park away from the canal, then you can do so as far as Roman Road, and from there enter Victoria Park. Mile End Park is fairly new, is landscaped in a natural fashion and has plenty of space for your dog to run about.

If you stay with us on the tow-path – it's wide enough to accommodate two dogs larking about – continue under a concrete bridge and past a lock. An attractive pub (the Royal Cricketers) on the opposite side of the canal has a waterside garden. There is a bridge just behind you which you can cross to reach it. Stay on the tow-path until you find, on your right, Victoria Park's Arcade Gate. Enter the park and turn right along a broad (but traffic-free road) which leads past the lake. Put your dog on the lead if he is prone to chase ducks, geese or swans – there are hordes of them about and lots of people feeding them. Amber dashed into the middle of one family and hoovered up all the bread they had scattered on the ground.

If you want to avoid the wildfowl, turn left and walk along the road until you reach two stone sentinel dogs. Turn right along the carriageway between them and skirt the lake, keeping it to your right. There are banks of shrubs on this shore to deflect your dog from the birds.

To reach Cambridge Heath BR

At the sentinel dogs turn left and exit the park through Bonner Gate. Like all the park's gates it sports a smart, blue notice-board with a potted history of the park on it.

Victoria Park was created in the nineteenth century because the area had a mortality rate far higher than the rest of London – as a result of overcrowding, unsanitary conditions and polluted air. Wrote the Registrar General of Births, Deaths and Marriages in 1839, 'A park in the east of London would probably diminish the deaths by thousands and add several years to the lives of the entire population.' It has to be said, however, that the powers that be weren't entirely altruistic. Sanitary reports cited evidence that epidemics tended to arise in the congested streets of east London, then travel to the West End – the area was a source of disease for the entire capital. It was also thought that a park might dissipate potential social unrest in the years of the Chartists – the Victorians must have known a thing or two about the calming effects of green spaces.

The Registrar's report was followed by a petition to Queen Victoria. She agreed with the proposal and the park's 290 acres (116 hectares) were laid out by James Pennethorne, a protege of John Nash. These days the park is a delight and clearly much loved by local people. The first time I was there an elderly man with a tiny scrap of a terrier in tow came up to me and announced, 'This is our park. Queen Victoria gave it to us.' Either royalty still has considerable clout in the East End, or the people of Hackney are tidy minded about litter, or the park keepers super zealous – whichever way it is, Victoria Park is a model of cleanliness and elegance. Yet the area in which is stands is just as deprived as that which surrounds the blighted acres of Burgess Park in Southwark (see Walk 15). And whereas the lake in Burgess Park is sinister and menacing, the one in Victoria Park is a delight – but more of the lake later.

At Bonner Gate put your dog on the lead, pass a superloo, cross Sewardstone Way, turn right, then left into Bishop's Way, left on Russia Lane, right on Parmiter Street and find, at Cambridge Heath Road, the BR station straight in front of you. If you prefer to go home via Bethnal Green tube, turn left and the station is only a short distance. It has an escalator I'm afraid.

To continue on the main route

Walk beside the lake, keeping it to your left. The park is flat throughout, but is made interesting by shrubs and trees. The lake is its centre-piece. It has soft contours and islands and a fountain the spray from which, in summer, reaches the shore as a cooling mist on your bare arms. On the bank on which we are walking is a border of flax plants which inspired, on an earlier excursion to the park, in different company, a fit of extreme covetousness in the keen gardener friend who was accompanying us. At the top of the lake is a cafe with white, wrought iron tables and chairs, white table-cloths, flowery cushions and a cool, grey-tiled floor. You can have afternoon tea with scones and cream here very cheaply. Dogs aren't allowed inside, of course, but they can sit beside the tables on the terrace and enjoy the view over the lake. There are loos in the cafe and, if you go round the back of it, you will discover an ice cream kiosk.

If you explore Victoria Park you will come across smart, royal blue, signposts. These direct you along the Bow Heritage Trail. The Trail isn't particularly good for dogs – it's too built up – but it is rich in history. One of the main things that strikes you when you walk it is the extent to which the inhabitants of the East End were forced to put up with all the unpleasant things which the wealthier NIMBYs of the West End couldn't bear to have in their neighbourhood. As early as Roman times cattle were brought here to be slaughtered, then their carcases carried into the city. During the plague of 1361 cows were slaughtered on one side of the city at Stratford and on the other at Knightsbridge, 'to keep the air free from filthy and putrid smells'. In his journal of the Great Plague of 1665, Daniel Defoe mentions that meat was butchered at Mile End and brought to the city's centre on the backs of horses.

In the nineteenth century industry came to the East End – all the 'bad neighbour' industries which, under Acts of Parliament, were not allowed in the wealthier areas of the capital. Oil-boilers, gut-spinners and varnish-makers invaded streets which had once been lined with the sumptuous, suburban residences of wealthy London merchants and professionals.

In the early 1850s the East End was chosen to syphon off the contents of the water closets of the West Enders (of which more later). These days it still suffers from chemical plants and industrial dereliction on a scale which would never be tolerated in Knightsbridge, or leafy Chiswick or on the fringes of Hampstead Heath.

But back to the pleasant greenery of Victoria Park. After the cafe, continue along the tarmac path sloppy right to the exit on Grove Road. Put your dog on the lead, turn left along the smart blue fencing and when it ends, cross the road, enter the next leg of Victoria Park and release your dog. This part of the park is flat, mown grass given over to ball games. Fred enjoyed one with his tennis balls. Go along the tarmac path past a blue bandstand and a large play area with rock formations for children to climb as though they were goats in London Zoo. To the left is a pond. It's deep and its bottom is thick in black slime – don't let your dog take the plunge, you will regret it! After the playground, turn right on the path to pass a fairly barren enclosure confining fallow deer, goats, chickens and a peahen or so. When you see a mural on a wall ahead, turn right to leave the park by Lockhouse Gate. Go along the approach road to push open a black wooden door to the right and join the tow-path beside the Hertford Union Canal. Turn left. The water is very deep, though, thank goodness, the banks are shallow. Don't risk leaving your dog loose if he is (a) exuberant (b) silly or (c) young enough and uncoordinated enough to make a mistake. The first time I did this walk I kept Fred on the lead. A year and a half later he was sensible enough to be trusted. But at the next lock eight month old Amber bent for a drink, her bum in the air, lost her balance and executed a classic pratfall, landing splat! in the deep water. It was okay, her owners soon hauled her out and, given her short coat, she didn't drench everyone in the vicinity as Fred does when he shakes after an unexpected dip. Nor – given her youth – did she look in the least embarrassed as Fred had when he took the plunge in the Grand Union near Willesden Junction (see Walk 18).

After the lock the path takes you under the motorway (the A102 (M)). Pass Upper Bottom Pumping Station, a lock and Lower Bottom Pumping Station to see the Lee Navigational Channel join the canal. At the black, humpbacked bridge on Carpenter's Road cross the Channel to the right.

To reach Hackney Wick BR

Put your dog on the lead at the bridge, turn left on White Post Lane and the station is to your right

To continue on the main route

Follow the Lee Valley signpost south towards Old Ford Lock. Its northern arm points to Hackney Marsh (see Walk 3). Here I would keep your dog on the lead unless he is a sedate, grey-muzzled, senior citizen canine and/or you want to see him swept away by strong currents. Or unless he's as sensible as Fred now is. At Old Ford Lock is a house with some very odd objects in its garden – a satellite dish, then several things you might recognise if you're a morning TV person. The first time I was there the garden was home to a doll's house too big for dolls; a giant milk bottle; a vast egg cup with a brown egg in it; two mugs the size of teenagers; and a huge tin of baked beans. The second time I was there a vast, spotty teapot poured a solid, brown, rubbery stream into umpteen cups and two speckled, black and white cockerels pecked around the place, cox combs wobbling. This is where The Big Breakfast is filmed. Immediately beyond the house, at a River Lee signpost, turn right across a lock gate and snap on your dog's lead as you enter deserted Dace Road with warehouses on either side. Like most empty London roads, this is L plate territory, so watch out for learner drivers mounting the pavements and stop-starting along the street. In a hundred metres or so, step up dingy steps to your left between red brick walls and release your dog. Turn left on the tarmac path. In winter the path has low, rank grass on either side – in summer it's a riot of dog roses and columbine. You are walking on top of the covered-over Northern Outfall Sewer (NOSE for short). The sewer was built following the 'Great Stink' of 1855. In those days the Thames was so polluted that if you fell into it you didn't drown, you were poisoned. When a paddle steamer passed, people scattered in panic to dodge the excreta it churned up. The stench became so bad that curtains drenched in chloride of lime had to be hung at the windows of the Houses of Parliament which faced the river and there was serious talk of moving Parliament out of London. Instead an Act of Parliament was passed which established the Metropolitan Board of Works and charged it with constructing a proper sewerage and drainage system. One of the results was the Northern Outfall Sewer.

As I say, in summer the path is a delight but in winter it is rather dull. But only for the moment. Go straight to cross the wide bridge over the confluence of two channels of water. A scrapyard to your right holds an incredible number of defunct cars. The landscape is an extraordinary scene of urban dereliction. It looks like a set from a science fiction movie in which Armageddon has come and gone and only sporadic signs of primitive life are visible in the wastelands of decay. Far away, to your right, is Canary Wharf, slightly nearer is a huge, red brick warehouse, its exterior as forbidding as that of a Victorian prison. Closer still are the roaring flames of a fire – lit by vagrants, wreckers, workmen trying to keep warm? This is the scene for which it's worth taking this walk – there's nothing like it elsewhere in the whole of London.

Utterly out of place in this surreal cityscape are the arty, pink perspex signs which direct you along the Greenway (which is what the embankment on the top of the Northern Outfall Sewer is now called). They are also very difficult to read. At a sign to Pudding Mill, descend the steps. We were there on a Sunday when there was no traffic on the road. On a weekday there might be lorries roaring up and down, delivering stuff or taking it away from still-functioning, industrial plants. But on Sunday you can safely leave a sober dog like Fred to trot along behind you.

At the road – which has a serious litter problem – *do not turn left.* We did and passed first a Rottweiler guarding some premises, then two German Shepherds struggling to attack us from beneath a corrugated iron fence. They had room to get out, I thought, and hurried past in a panic, condemning myself for a wimp. But it turned out that the entire party (except for Amber, she carried on blithely in her innocent, puppyish way) had been thoroughly rattled by the encounter. To avoid it, when you leave the sewer embankment, go straight across the road ahead, take the branch to the left, past THE CAFE (well advertised on the walls around, but closed when we were there), to find a Greenway sign and follow it to the left. Pudding Mill station (DLR) is on the lane.

. . . *two German Shepherds struggling to attack us from beneath a corrugated iron fence.*

When you reach Pudding Mill Lane (to your left), there may be roadworks – but there is still pedestrian access to ghastly, busy Stratford High Street. Or the construction work may be over, in which case you can turn left after you cross the river and walk along the tow-path to Blaker Road. From there, put your dog on the lead, turn right, follow Blaker Road to the right to Stratford High Street, cross it by the subway, go down Abbey Lane straight ahead to find, in a few metres, Abbey Lane Open Space on the left. Enter it and release your dog. Follow the tarmac path, passing a pylon to your left, to find – again to your left – stairs and/or a concrete slope which lead to the gravelled Greenway.

To reach West Ham

From here you can walk all the way to West Ham, crossing a minimum of roads, digressing to the south in a loop between Clock Mill and Distillery to follow the Long Wall, cross the footbridge over Prescott Channel, bear to the right and follow the path between a concrete fence and the Channelsea River. You will pass the Abbey Mills Pumping Station, built in 1865 and now a listed building. Pass Abbey Creek Island to find the steps which return you to the Greenway. In fact, on the Greenway, you can walk all the way to Becktcn and from there explore Beckton District Park or the Alps. Newham Council have leaflets with details of these walks.

But we didn't try them. When we reached the Greenway at Abbey Lane, we were tired; the chill, spring mist was thickening; and our dogs had had a fine time. So we turned for home. Back along Marshgate Lane to the Greenway, back down Dace Street to the headquarters of the Big Breakfast Show. I looked longingly at the path which led south east beside the river but thought – I can always come back another day to explore that. Back to Victoria Park – but don't go into it. Ignore the black door, instead pass a row of pretty cottages and continue along the tow-path.

Throughout the entire walk we had come across no bins for dog waste. Now Fred did a number and I scooped it into a plastic bag and pressed on. I ended up carrying it for nigh on ten minutes. There wasn't even a litter bin in which to deposit it, for God's sake. So where do people put their litter, let alone their dog's mess? Well, what they do with it is they throw it on the ground – and as for their dogs, they let them do their business all over the path. Several times we stepped around the messy evidence, or remarked on heavy accumulations of soft drink cans, scraps of paper and empty crisp packets. It's all very well for local authorities to inveigh against litter and the harmful effects of dog mess, but if there's nowhere to put it, what are you supposed to do?

Thankfully, we reached the edge of Victoria Park, which has lots of bins. Press on along the canal. When you reach the Royal Cricketers pub, turn left along the tow-path, press on as for the outward journey, leave the path by the blue gate through which you entered and cross Mile End Park to return to Mile End tube. Fred was fairly knackered after his games with Amber. I bet your dog will have a good time too.

Walk 20: Green Chain

This excursion follows the middle section of the Green Chain Walk which covers 40 miles through open spaces in south east London. The Chain is a credit to the boroughs involved – Greenwich, Lewisham, Bexley and Bromley – and the bits I don't cover here are described in leaflets available from them: or you can set out from any of the parks or stations I mention and follow the Green Chain signs.

This walk is a six-mile trip ideal for dogs and for people who enjoy woodland, commons, views unrivalled in the rest of the city and the delightful treat of open farmland, with no farm animals to excite your dog. Wherever you live in London it's as well worth a day out as a trip to, say, Brighton or the North Downs. Connects with Walk 15.

Route: Charlton BR or Woolwich Dockyard BR circular walk with diversions to Falconwood BR, Welling BR, Plumstead BR, Abbey Wood BR, Belvedere BR, Erith BR, Eltham BR, Mottingham BR, Grove Park BR, Elmstead Woods BR, Sunridge Park BR, Ravensbourne BR, Lower Sydenham BR, Beckenham Hill BR, New Beckenham BR, Kent House BR, Penge East BR and Crystal Palace BR. There is an extension walk to Petts Wood BR.

Distance: 10½ miles

Facilities: Pubs with gardens along the route. Seasonal park cafes in Maryon Park, Oxleas Wood, Lesnes Abbey Woods, Eltham Park, Avery Hill Park, Chinbrook Meadows and Beckenham Palace Park. Loos in Maryon Wilson Park, Oxleas Wood, Bostall Wood, just to the south of Plumstead Common, Mottingham Sports Ground, Grove Park, Beckenham Palace Park, Cator Park and Crystal Palace Park.

From Charlton BR

Cross Charlton Church Lane and follow Floyd Road, Harvey Gardens and Coxmount Road to Maryon Wilson Park. You are now on the Green Chain. In fact this section begins at the Thames Barrier and brings you down through Maryon Park. The Maryon-Wilsons were lords of the manor of Charlton for over 200 years and they gave the two parks to the public. Both used to be part of Hanging Wood which provided shelter for the highwaymen of Shooters Hill and Blackheath. Follow the Green Chain signs to Charlton Park and the Green Chain 'major signpost'. Turn right, follow the path to the end and turn left. In Charlton Park you might want to look at Charlton House – considered by experts one of the best examples of Jacobean architecture in the country and the finest in London. It's a short detour right and then left from the point on which you now stand. Otherwise follow the marker posts to leave the park at the gate leading into Charlton Park Lane. Put your dog on the lead. Turn right, cross Canberra Road and turn left into Inigo Jones Road. At the end of it enter Hornfair Park and release your dog. It's a small park which was once the venue of the annual Horn Fair at which men carried horns or wore them on their heads. There was a procession from the riverside to the church around which the crowd marched three times, then 'fell to lecherie and songs, daunces, harping, piping and also to glotony and sinne'.

Instead of doing that follow the path left, around the play area, and left again to a narrow path. Bear right through the gate to emerge on Stadium Road. Put your dog on the lead. Turn left, bear right onto Woolwich Common and release your dog. Just before Academy Road turn right when paths cross (watch your dog, traffic isn't far away) and then bear left. Put your dog on the lead and emerge on Academy Road near the covered reservoir. Cross Academy Road, turn right and walk its length to cross Shooters Hill at the traffic lights. Turn left and just past the police station go right to enter Eltham Common. Release your dog.

Eltham Common, Castle Wood, Jack Wood, Oxleas Woods and Shepherdleas Wood together cover 325 acres (130 hectares). Head down the hill to a Green Chain marker post. Turn left. The path will lead you to Severndroog Castle. It isn't a castle, it's a summer-house built in 1784 by a widow in memory of her husband Sir William James, to mark his conquest, as commander of marine forces, of the Castle of Severndroog on the coast of Malabar. It's a fine, imposing tower, which is now empty. Go behind the castle (doesn't matter which side) and down the steps to a rose garden. Below it is

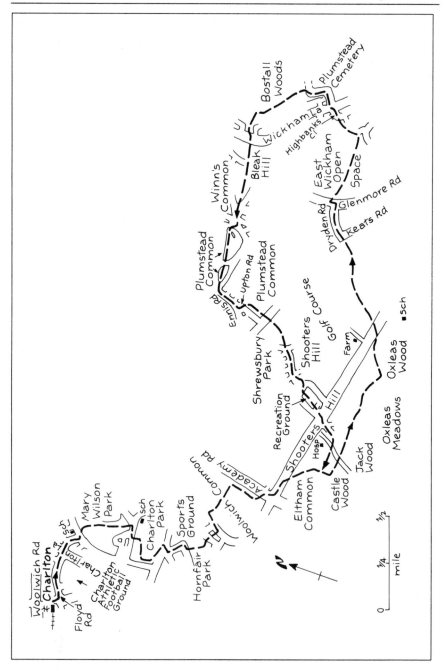

grassland and a panoramic view of south London. If you want you can explore Castle Wood and Jack Wood below you; or have a picnic as I and my companion did.

Follow the path (and a waymark) to your left into the woods. You will emerge from them in front of more rose gardens. There are loos here. There's a drinking fountain too, but no tray round its base from which dogs can lap. I was glad I'd brought a bottle of water for Fred and a plastic bowl. Take the right fork leading downhill, following the Green Chain sign, and go through the woods to the very large, green, open space of Oxleas Meadows. Good views here too. Turn left up the hill to the Green Chain signpost, right in front of the cafe and plunge back into the woods. Turn left at a Green Chain sign along a wide, woodland walk. You will soon hear the heavy traffic on Shooters Hill, but you don't need to put your dog on the lead until you see the road in front of you. Or at least you don't if your dog can be trusted, as Fred now can, to stop in his tracks at a whistle and a call of 'Wait!'.

Cross busy Shooters Hill and turn right. Ignore the opening into farmland on your left – there's a notice explaining that it's private. Opposite the Green Chain signpost on the other side of the road, turn left and release your dog. So far the paths have been surfaced. Now you're on a rough, trodden track between blackberries and tall, rough grass, filled with the noisy doings of umpteen insects. To your left is a stream and a hedgerow which is a tangle of elder, hawthorn, osier and crab ·apple. Press on into a wide, open field, turn right along the hedgerow and right again into the next field. These fields belong to the closest working farm to central London (you're no more than seven or eight miles from the centre here). The fields supply barley for pig feed and straw for bedding. Follow the footpath half left to the brow of the hill, then towards a metal paling fence. Go through a gap in the hedgerow, then through a swing gate and pass a Green Chain waymark beside a stream to your left. When you see Dryden Road ahead (it's a quiet, suburban street) put your dog on the lead and press straight ahead, following the Green Chain signs. At the end of Dryden Road, turn left into Glenmore Road and cross it to enter East Wickham Open Space. Release your dog.

Go straight along a wide, green mown path beneath a beguiling mix of trees. East Wickham Open Space was once a council tip. Now it's a very big green expanse with views over allotments and Woolwich Cemetery to your left and a church spire ahead which led my human companion to reminisce about her childhood in the countryside of Somerset. We came across a small bird of prey on the path which took off in leisurely, unfazed fashion at Fred's approach.

To reach Welling BR

When you enter East Wickham Open Space strike across it to the right to find Rippersley Road. Put your dog on the lead. At the end of Rippersley Road turn right into Wickham Street, left into Central Avenue and left again into Station Approach.

To continue on the main route

At another metal paling put your dog on the lead. Emerge on Highbanks Road and walk straight ahead to the junction. The Forester's Arms has chairs and tables outside. Cross busy Wickham Lane, turn left, then right up Cemetery Road beside Plumstead Cemetery. Follow the tarmac track as it veers left and – as long as your dog can be called out of the path of the rare car which travels the lane – you can release him. At Woodside Cottage plunge straight ahead into Bostall Woods. They are lovely and – combined with Bostall Heath and Lesnes Abbey Wood – cover 137 hectares. Dick Turpin is thought to have used them as a refuge from the king's troops.

To reach Erith BR

Follow the Green Chain signs on the long trek through Lesnes Abbey Woods and Franks Park. Belvedere BR is adjacent to the route.

To continue on the main route

Ignore the next Green Chain arrow and press straight ahead. Walk beside an iron railing to your left, then follow the path which bears away from it to the right and climb a steep hill, courtesy of steps made by logs. At the top, take the wide path to the left. Turn left again at the next junction. Ignore all turnings to the left which lead to roads until – about ten metres before allotments – find a waymark post, half-hidden in the undergrowth. Go down the steps to the left

Between blackberries and tall, rough grass, filled with the noisy doings of umpteen insects.

to a grassy expanse between high, wire-mesh fences and take the exit to the left. Be careful as you approach the busy road ahead (Wickham Lane) because it isn't fenced.

Put your dog on the lead, turn right, cross Wickham Lane, enter the footpath straight ahead and release him. You are on inappropriately-named Bleak Hill. It's a charming ascent (though marred by rubbish on its lower slopes) through bracken to the top of the hill; and a surprising return to urban landscapes. You are on flat, dull Winn's Common. There's a Green Chain signpost beside you. Don't follow any of its arms; instead head straight across the common (watch your dog doesn't join in a football game) to its apex where three roads (King's Highway, Winn's Common Road and Lakedale Road) meet. The best thing about the common is the shop on the other side of King's Highway which not only sells real fruit juice ice lollies but will provide water for your dog as long as you have a bottle and a bowl.

To reach Plumstead BR

Head straight up Lakedale Road to turn left on Plumstead High Street. You should reach the station in another ten minutes.

To continue on the main route

Go left, then cross The Slade as soon as possible. Take a couple of steps along The Slade, turn onto the steps which lead down. Release your dog. At the bottom, climb the steep steps and emerge on Plumstead Common. Keep to the north of it, passing a couple of pubs with tables outside. Follow Old Mill Road as it runs to the north of the common – watch out for your dog as traffic is close. At the junction with Plumstead Common Road put him on the lead and cross into Ennis Road.

To reach Woolwich Arsenal BR

Stay on Plumstead Common Road and walk past another section of the common to turn right at Sandy Hill Road, right again into Brookhill Road and right once more into Woolwich New Road to find the station.

To continue on the main route

Take the curves of the road in your stride past Macoma Road and Tuam Road until you come upon a Green Chain sign directing you left. Don't release your dog as you climb the steps. Emerge on Upton Road, turn left and, after the bend to the right, bear left again to more steps. Release your dog. Climb the steps to find a hayfield to your right and allotments to your left. You are on Shooters Hill. The hill is 432 feet (131m) high and was once the haunt of highwaymen.

Now head downhill to the Green Chain waymark. Cross Dothill Road (which is an unmade track) and press on up again across Shrewsbury Park. It isn't a park, it's a meadow dotted with trees. At the next Green Chain waymark ignore the arrow which suggests you go straight ahead and turn half left across the grass. Now stop. And look at the view! The City, the countryside of Essex are laid out below you. At the corner of Shrewsbury Park (next to a red dog mess bin), find an enclosed path with a Green Chain waymark at its entrance. There's a fenced golf course to your left and fenced gardens to your right, so no need to put your dog on the lead yet.

Do so when you emerge into pretty Mereworth Drive. Hereabouts the householders don't just tend their own gardens, they also cultivate a narrow strip beside the kerb. Turn left along Kinlet Road and Castlefield Road to Foxcroft Road. Cross to the right onto Eaglefield Recreation Ground, release your dog and go straight ahead (ignoring the Green Chain signpost) up the hill to the playground. Circuit the playground to the left to reach Cleanthus Road. Put your dog on the lead, turn left and walk to the short footpath which leads beside a red brick water-tower and two pretty cottages. The water tower was completed in 1910 and is a landmark for many miles around.

Cross the main road with your dog still on the lead and enter Kenilworth Gardens. Follow the Green Chain marker left down Crown Woods Lane. At a pretty cottage turn right into the depths of Oxleas Woods and find yourself back on the track from which you started. Release your dog. From here make your way back across Woolwich Common to the station from which you set out or go south east across Shepherdleas Wood to find Falconwood BR.

To reach Crystal Palace BR (and join Walk 15)

Follow the Green Chain signs south from Oxleas Wood. You will pass through Eltham Park North, Eltham Park South, Avery Hill Park (in which the river Shuttle puts in a small appearance, shaded by hawthorns), Mottingham Sports Ground, Elmstead Wood, Sunridge Park, Beckenham Place Park and Cator Park. An alternative route leads from Mottingham BR south through Chinbrook Meadows and Marvels Wood to join the main walk in Sunridge Park. Look out for the Quaggy River in Sunridge Park and for the Ravensbourne (Pool) in Beckenham Place Park.

BR stations en route are Eltham, New Eltham, Mottingham, Grove Park, Elmstead Woods, Sunridge Park, Ravensbourne, Beckenham Hill, New Beckenham, Lower Sydenham, Kent House, Penge East and Penge West.

Further north you can walk in linear parks beside the Ravensbourne, passing Catford BR, Ladywell BR and Lewisham BR almost clear to Greenwich where, of course, you and your dog can explore the 180 hectares of Greenwich Park and Blackeath. But that's another story and one I don't have room for here.

P.S. A horizontal arm of the Green Chain leads from Elmstead Woods to Chislehurst along an unnamed footpath and across Whyte's Woodland. From there, if you cross Chislehurst Common, you are only a short distance from the extensive green complex of Scadbury Park, Petts Wood and Jubilee Country Park in which you can walk for hours and have only one road to cross. Petts Wood BR is a short walk from the south east corner of Jubilee Country Park. Phone Bromley Council on 0181 464 3333 ext 3526 for leaflets about these parks.

Tube and BR stations

Parks, paths, lakes and rivers

Also of Interest:

TEA SHOP WALKS IN THE CHILTERNS

Jean Patefield lives in High Wycombe and her book is packed with easy walks that can be enjoyed by all the family - especially with the prospect of afternoon tea! £6.95

RAILWAY RAMBLES: London & the South-East

Clive Higgs, a lifelong Londoner who has always declined to own a car, describes a selection of attractive rambles that can be easily reached on the network of trains running from central London. **"Get down to the booking office now"** FARNHAM HERALD. £4.95

BEST PUB WALKS IN AND AROUND CENTRAL LONDON

Discover London on foot, and pop into one or more of its famous hostelries. The pubs are packed with history and there's much to see on Ruth Herman's entertaining romp (and stagger?) around the streets of London. £6.95